I, Michel Foucault...

To find the real Michel Foucault is to ask "which one"?

Should we look at the life of the man himself, who as a boy wanted to be a goldfish, but became a philosopher and historian, political activist, leather queen, bestseller, tireless campaigner for dissident causes?

Do not ask who I am and do not ask me to remain the same.

What about his literary skill, combined with painstaking historical inquiry, his excellence as a pasta cook, captivating lecturing style, passion for sex with men, occasional drug-taking, barbed sense of humour, competitiveness, fierce temper – and the fact that he came from a family of doctors and dearly loved his mother?

Foucault the Author?

Or should we see Michel Foucault as the **author**, whose work combines brilliant insight and eccentric detail, uniting contemporary philosophical practice with the archaeology of the many documents he patiently retrieved from history? And what should we exclude, given the huge shifts in theoretical position over his career?

Foucault himself problematized the meaning of **authorship** – a function, he claimed, which resolved or hid many contradictions.

We must dispense with our habit of looking for an author's authority, and show instead how the power of discourse constrains both author and his utterances.

So Foucault was reluctant to write his own biography or have someone do it for him. But many have, since his death.

Foucault

FOR BEGINNERS

Chris Horrocks and Zoran Jevtic

Edited by Richard Appignanesi

ICON ❖ BOOKS

Published in 1997 by Icon Books Ltd.,
Grange Road, Duxford, Cambridge CB2 4QF

Distributed in the UK, Europe, Canada, South Africa and Asia
by the Penguin Group:
Penguin Books Ltd., 27 Wrights Lane, London W8 5TZ

Published in Australia in 1997 by Allen & Unwin Pty. Ltd.,
PO Box 8500, 9 Atchison Street, St. Leonards, NSW 2065

Originating editor: Richard Appignanesi

ISBN 1 874166 54 4

Printed and bound in Great Britain by
Biddles Ltd., Guildford and King's Lynn

A Transdiscursive Man

Foucault gave us the term **transdiscursive**, which describes how, for example, Foucault is not simply an author of a book, but the author of a theory, tradition or discipline.

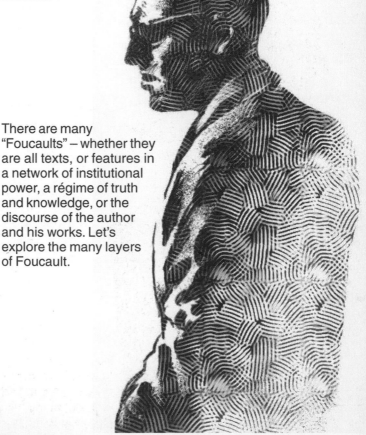

We can at least say that he was the instigator of a method of historical inquiry which has had major effects on the study of subjectivity, power, knowledge, discourse, history, sexuality, madness, the penal system and much else. Hence the term, "**Foucaldian**".

There are many "Foucaults" – whether they are all texts, or features in a network of institutional power, a régime of truth and knowledge, or the discourse of the author and his works. Let's explore the many layers of Foucault.

Foucault's Project

Foucault sought to account for the way in which human beings have *historically* become the **subject** and **object** of political, scientific, economic, philosophical, legal and social discourses and practices.

But Foucault does not take the idea of subjectivity in philosophical isolation. It becomes linked with – and even produced by **knowledge** and **power** through – **dividing practices** where, for example, psychiatry divides the mad from the sane.

Scientific classification: where science classifies the individual as the subject of life (biology), labour (economics) and language (linguistics).

Subjectification: the way the individual turns himself into a subject of health, sexuality, conduct, etc.

My fundamental question: "What form of reason, and which historical conditions, led to this?"

Foucault Fiction

"In my books I do like to make fictional use of the materials I assemble or put together, and I deliberately make fictional constructions with authentic elements."

Let's "fictionalize" Foucault's life by turning it into a biographical account of Foucault and his *oeuvre* or work.

He was born Paul-Michel Foucault, on 15 October 1926, to Anne Malapert and wealthy surgeon Paul Foucault, in conservative Poitiers in France. Paul-Michel Foucault had a sister Francine and a younger brother, Denys.

Each of my works is a part of my own biography.

Foucault had brown hair, a big nose and blue eyes. Foucault didn't like the name Paul-Michel, because nasty children made it sound like Polichinello (Punch)!
He changed it to Michel – perhaps expressing love for his Mum, who'd insisted on the name at his birth.

Camp Catholics and Choirboys

Foucault was of the Catholic faith. Later, he said he enjoyed its camp ritual. He was even a choirboy for a while.

1930. Paul-Michel was enrolled early in elementary class at the Lycée Henri-IV.

He moved into the Lycée proper in 1932 and remained there until 1936 – the year he saw refugees arriving from the Spanish Civil War.

He was an enthusiastic cyclist and tennis player, but he was short-sighted, and often missed the ball. He enjoyed trips to the theatre, and occasionally the cinema.

Because I want to be with my sister.

He was a young and disciplined student. Knowledge meant social promotion for his class.

A perfect bourgeois childhood ... or was it?

Seen my new shoes anywhere, Michel?

WAR!

1 Sept 1939: France falls to the Nazis, and her troops retreat south. Poitiers becomes a medical centre.

17 June 1940: Prime Minister Pétain requests armistice. Germans use the Foucaults' holiday home as officers' billet. Foucault steals firewood for school from collaborationist militia. Foucault does well at school, but messes up his summer exams in 1940.

I blame my failure on World War II, and the subsequent influx of other pupils from better schools!

He transfers to the religious Collège Saint-Stanislas and gains prizes in French, history, Greek and English.

1942: Begins formal study in philosophy.

June 1943: Passes his *baccalauréat*. Argues with his father about his career. Medicine? Michel Foucault thought not – he wanted to go to the prestigious academic hothouse, the ENS (École Normale Supérieure) in Paris.

Paris – The Top 100

After two years' study, he took the ENS entrance exam. He had to be in the top 100 to go to the oral exam. He came 101st! But parental influence gained him entry to the Lycée Henri IV in Paris' Latin Quarter. Foucault was on his way to Paris …

Foucault loved studying history, but Hyppolite showed him that philosophy could explain history.

But is history just a patient progress towards reason, and does philosophy have limits?

Georg Wilhelm Friedrich Hegel (1770-1831)

Hegel thought that what is real is rational, and that the truth is "the whole" – one great, complex system which he called the **Absolute**. He believed that Mind or **Spirit** was the ultimate reality. Mind has an ever-expanding consciousness of itself, and philosophy allows us to develop self-awareness of the whole and free ourselves from the **unreason** and contradiction of partial knowledge.

Reason is the Sovereign of the World ... the history of the world, therefore, presents us with a rational process.

Hyppolite and Hegel

A modern reading of Hegel shows us that philosophy cannot see itself as a view of history which can achieve completion, but an endless task carried out against the backdrop of an infinite horizon!

Philosopher **Alexandre Kojève** (1900-68) had also rescued Hegel from the Romantic view of him as the lumbering creator of systems.

Hegel was now modern!

This "Frenchified" Hegel had a new cutting edge.

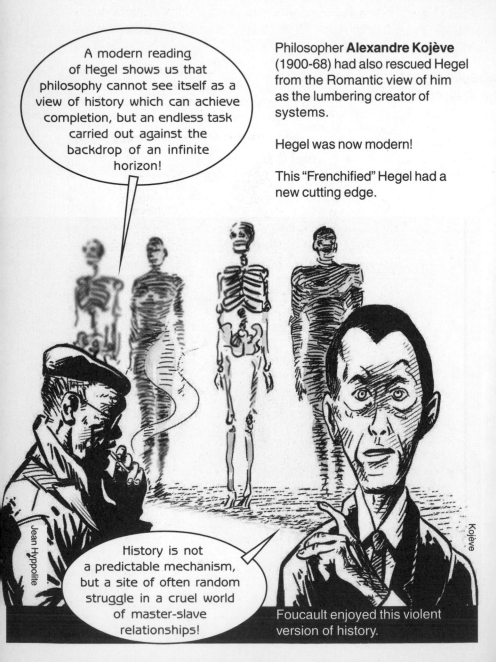

Jean Hyppolite

Kojève

History is not a predictable mechanism, but a site of often random struggle in a cruel world of master-slave relationships!

Foucault enjoyed this violent version of history.

The Return of Hegel

Hegel had started the attempt to explore the **irrational** and to integrate it into an expanded reason. But was this still part of the modern task of philosophy – the search for a total system which would absorb **un**reason?

I appreciated the issues Hegel raised, but was not interested in providing a general theory of history. I left that to Marxists.

Foucault was not rejecting **reason** as such, but he did refuse to see it as a "way out" or inevitable outcome of history. His engagement with philosophy is not to provide a system for the conditions in which knowledge or truth is possible or reliable (as Kant did), but to examine what reason's historical effects are, where its limits lie, and what price it exacts.

Foucault the Student

In July 1946 Foucault took his entrance exam. He came fourth. The ENS beckoned!

Life at the ENS was tough. Foucault was unsociable, argumentative, unhealthy and given to depression. The fiercely competitive environment of this prestigious school didn't help. Yet Foucault worked intensely. His fellows hated him and thought him mad.

He slashed his chest with a razor, pursued a student while wielding a dagger and tried to kill himself with pills in 1948. He encountered institutional psychiatry for the first time.

Gay Foucault

It wasn't all tears, though. Foucault was a practical joker and an excellent duellist with a wet towel. He even climbed the roofs and once stole a book from a store (wow!). His nickname was "Fuchs" – Fox – on account of his sharp features and high intelligence.

I was gay and sexually active in my late adolescence. But I had to be discreet about my love of men.

Sexual scandal ruined careers. Oppressive laws dictated that it was even an offence for men to dance together in a public environment. His secret life would later explode in his writing on **transgression**, sexuality, pleasure and the body.

Philosophical Currents...

Foucault was interested in two dominant brands of philosophy in France.

The philosophies of experience, the subject, meaning and consciousness – **existentialism** and **phenomenology**.

The work of existentialist **Jean-Paul Sartre** (1905-80) asks what it is to exist as a human being, how individuals experience their existence, how they make choices and deal with freedom and authenticity.

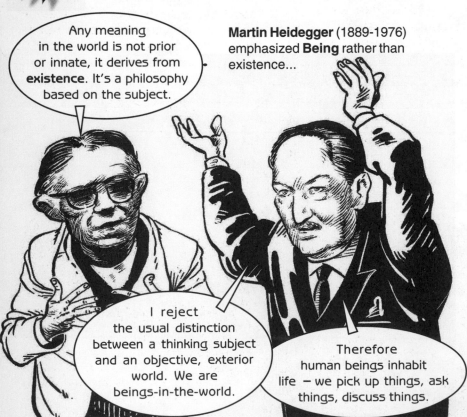

Any meaning in the world is not prior or innate, it derives from **existence**. It's a philosophy based on the subject.

Martin Heidegger (1889-1976) emphasized **Being** rather than existence...

I reject the usual distinction between a thinking subject and an objective, exterior world. We are beings-in-the-world.

Therefore human beings inhabit life – we pick up things, ask things, discuss things.

Foucault would see how this *Dasein* analysis could provide a tool whereby the Being of a psychiatric patient, for example, is central to an understanding of the psychiatric world.

... and Phenomenology

Phenomenology is the investigation of the way that things – objects, images, ideas, emotions – appear or are present in our **consciousness**.

Phenomenology does this *without* reference to the status of objects outside our consciousness of them. It suspends the object "in itself", and only looks at our **experiencing** of it.

Some versions of *pure* phenomenology, such as that of **Edmund Husserl** (1859-1938), seek the grounds of human knowledge.

We must exclude all assumptions and theories about the contents of consciousness in order to discover innate structures or forms of consciousness which constitute all possibilities of mental experiences.

The phenomenology of **Maurice Merleau-Ponty** (1908-61) attempts to **describe** the perceptions of individuals as they experience space, colour and light.

Phenomenologists have no interest in explanations. They want the **immediate** experience!

Science and its Epistemology

The history and philosophy of science.

Epistemology is the theory of knowledge. The discipline examines what is knowable, what should count as knowledge and whether knowledge is certain in fields including science.

Gaston Bachelard (1884-1962) and **Alexandre Koyré** (1892-1964), philosophers and historians of science, stressed the role of **concept**, **system** and **structure** rather than lived consciousness or consciousness reflected in the world.

Truth as Activity

They considered science and knowledge not as objective or constant **truths**, but more as **discontinuous** "community" activities which constructed truth. While Bachelard stressed the problems of scientific practice, Koyré dismissed the idea that theories were objectively valid.

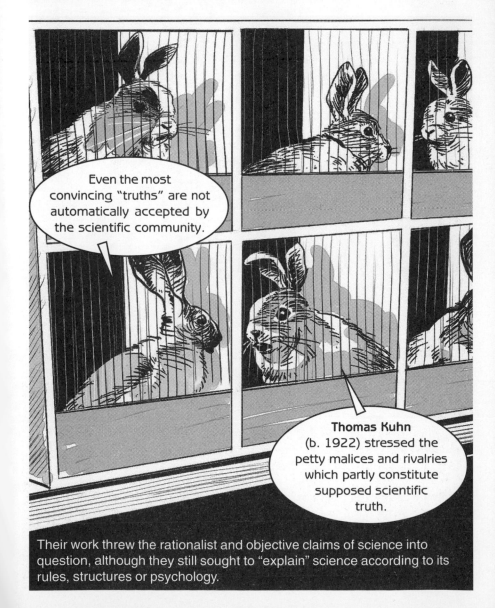

Their work threw the rationalist and objective claims of science into question, although they still sought to "explain" science according to its rules, structures or psychology.

"Cang"

I asked a simple question: "What is psychology? Is this science?"

I owed a great debt to my examiner and later close friend, the historian of science **Georges Canguilhem** (1904-95).

Canguilhem attacked the blindness of psychology to its own conditions – the grounds on and by which it constructs knowledge.

Psychologists are incapable of coherently defining the object of their study. Psychology is composite empiricism, codified in literary fashion for teaching purposes – and it's a police discipline.

Science is an exploration of rationality at work, but this should be seen **historically**.

Scientific truths are open to argument, but no less "real" because of their contingency. So scientific knowledge is seen as organized, operational and subject to change. It does not simply exist "out there".

Foucault's Project Takes Shape

Foucault's idea was to take some of the terms and methods of the history of science and apply them to another philosophical object – the **human subject**.

Foucault was unhappy with studying experience as the ground for knowledge on its own. It was too centred on the subject and assumed one could get back to prior or innate structures of meaning.

So, Foucault defined experience – for example, of madness or sexuality – in terms of the *experience* of individuals as *historically* based and the way in which this experience was grounded in philosophical and scientific discourse.

Foucault's History of Experience

Foucault made the link. No longer would history be opposed to experience.

I wondered whether it would not be possible to consider the very historicity of forms of experience.

The history of experience brings together Foucault the **historian** and Foucault the **philosopher**. Philosophy was not an inquiry into itself, but an application of philosophy to the human sciences: linguistics, psychology, sociology. How was it that knowledge and experience were incorporated into an apparently objective view of man as object? If we cannot take experience as a given truth, perhaps the questioning of scientific method can force us to ask: under which circumstances should we see any knowledge (of self or world) as tenable? What other factors apply?

It would be several years before these interests came to fruition in Foucault's work. Meanwhile, he kept studying.

Political Currents

Foucault joined the Parti Communiste Français (PCF) in 1950 at the suggestion of depressive Marxist mentor, **Louis Althusser** (1918-90). This was a Stalinist party at its most powerful because it still enjoyed credibility from its activities in the wartime Resistance.

He was not very committed and rarely attended meetings.

Althusser

I lazily adopted the Marxist belief that economic conditions determine social and political life, but was critical of the PCF's anti-Semitic propaganda and the sinister "proletarian" scientific doctrines it supported.

Such as? Stalinist biologist **T.D. Lysenko** (1898-1976) who believed that characteristics in the biological world were inherited and determined.

Foucault was beginning to see that scientific knowledge was linked to **power** rather than **truth**.

And according to Party dogma, his homosexuality would have been aligned with "bourgeois decadence".

Foucault Blows It

In spring 1950, Foucault took his final exams and passed the written stage. But his oral on "hypotheses" let him down. He had tried to show off!

In 1951, he finally passed but he was furious that he had to speak on "sexuality" in his oral. Little did he know how important this subject was to become …

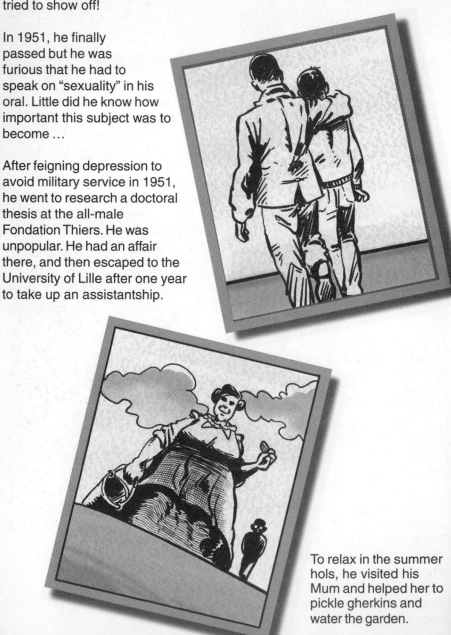

After feigning depression to avoid military service in 1951, he went to research a doctoral thesis at the all-male Fondation Thiers. He was unpopular. He had an affair there, and then escaped to the University of Lille after one year to take up an assistantship.

To relax in the summer hols, he visited his Mum and helped her to pickle gherkins and water the garden.

Towards Psychology?

Daniel Lagache (1903-72), who created the first French degree in psychology in 1947, and whose lectures Foucault attended, had persuaded him to take a psychology course in 1949. Foucault attended talks by **Georges Daumézon**, a founder of institutional psychotherapy, and psychoanalyst **Jacques Lacan** (1901-81).

At this point, I hadn't yet founded psychoanalysis on linguistic theories.
I was presenting my ideas on **identification** by referring to the proclivities of locusts and sticklebacks.

Hey, you're a locust, and you, and you...

Lacan

Foucault had been visiting Saint-Anne, the Paris psychiatric hospital. He had grown interested in the "rational" basis for research — this basis had to be questioned.

He also grew obsessed with Rorschach tests and tried them out on college mates. "That way, I'll know what's on their minds."

Experimental Dreams?

Foucault had an uneasy relationship to experimental psychology. He thought that the research of **Jacqueline Verdeaux** – psychiatrist and friend of the family – on the breathing rhythms of people listening to the "Symphony of Psalms" was ridiculous, as were Lacan's philosophical pretensions.

Yet he did assist Verdeaux in a translation and introduction to *Dream and Existence* by **Ludwig Binswanger** (1881-1966). This was closer to Foucault's concerns. It was *Dasein Analyse* – Heideggerian existential psychotherapy. Binswanger says:

A dream is nothing other than a particular mode of human existence in general, not a fulfilment of a wish, but of fundamental structures.

To dream of falling actually means our existence is falling and suffering. Dreams are to be taken literally.

I believe existential analysis helped me limit and better define what it was about academic psychiatric knowledge that was heavy and oppressive.

Psychology meets Heidegger

Written in 1953, Foucault's *Psychology from 1850 to 1950* reflected his attempts to resolve psychology's status as a science with its object – human existence.

Foucault claimed that the history of psychology is contradictory: it wants to be an objective science – like biology – but realizes that human reality is not simply a part of "natural objectivity".

How does one put "experience" under a microscope?

Psychology will be possible only if it marks a return to man's conditions of existence and to what is most human in man, namely his history.

Mental Illness and Psychology (1954) was published by Foucault to try to resolve different psychological methods – phenomenological, existential, Marxist.

Illness and Marx

In this Marxist reading, madness is a consequence of **alienation** from oneself and history, because material conditions are unresolvable.

It is not because one is ill that one is alienated, but because one is alienated one is ill.

The social relations determined by the present economy, in the guise of competition, exploitation, imperialist wars and class struggle, provide man with an experience of his human environment that is constantly haunted by contradiction.

To transform relations in the social environment would resolve illness at a stroke.

Foucault was denying that mental illness should be seen in negative terms, and stated that while psychology had moved from discussing evolution (science) to man (history), it still relied on "metaphysical" or moral prejudices.

Love on the Rocks

In the early 1950s, Foucault was moving in the same circles as the young musical genius **Pierre Boulez** (b. 1925). He also met and had a passionate affair with **Jean Barraqué** (1928-73), a young composer. They shared a taste for Heidegger and Nietzsche. Foucault gave him literary ideas to turn into music.

He knew historian **Paul Veyne** (b. 1930), who would later become a huge influence on Foucault's history of sexuality.

Veyne found Foucault too misogynistic, while Foucault thought Veyne's heterosexuality was a bore!

In December 1955, Foucault returned to Paris for Christmas. The love affair with Barraqué was in poor shape.

Listen to me, leave Foucault for your own good... This man will destroy you when he has destroyed himself.

You're right, I'll leave him!

Barraqué

29

Sweden!

In August 1955, Foucault was invited to apply to the Department of Romance Studies at the University of Uppsala in Sweden, at the recommendation of **Georges Dumézil** – "*le professeur*" – (1898-1986), specialist in Indo-European religions and mythologies. Dumézil employed an early form of **structuralism**.

His work concentrated on sets of universal, unchanging relations between and within cultures.

Foucault became French assistant and taught language and literature. He was also appointed director of the Maison de France as a cultural diplomat.

He thought Sweden would be socially less prohibitive than France, but the University was very strict, and the nightlife subdued.

Life is boring...

Foucault later said a certain kind of freedom could be as restrictive as a directly repressive society.

Foucault the Boozer

Foucault was a great cook, and entertained friends. He also drank heavily to compensate for the long dark nights, and cruised men.

He bought a brown Jaguar sports car – using cash from his family – which he sometimes drove into ditches because he was so pissed. There were frequent trips to Stockholm, where he enjoyed the company, stories and songs of the suave **Maurice Chevalier** (1888-1972).

He lectured on "The Conception of Love in French Literature from the Marquis de Sade to Jean Genet", to mainly female students.

I invited guest speakers to the Maison de France, including semiologist **Roland Barthes** (1915-80).

At this stage of my career, I was a freelance writer. Foucault and I became close friends – and occasional lovers.

Uppsala Library – The Birth of Madness

Foucault's Indiscretions

Foucault moved to Warsaw to run the Centre Français. Poland functioned badly. It had not recovered from World War II. Foucault wrote by candlelight. Politics was oppressive.

In 1957, students rioted against the suppression of the press, and Party membership declined.

In this climate of suspicion, Foucault fucked a young man who was working for the police to pay for his university education. Foucault was advised by the ambassador to leave Warsaw.

Mudwrestling

Foucault travelled with a lady inspector from the Ministry of Education on a visit to Cracow. She inadvertently barged into the Fox's bedroom – to find him in the arms of a young bloke.

Foucault later claimed this episode prevented him from stopping the events of the French student riots of May 1968, because the Ministry of Education did not take his reform plans seriously!

He moved to Hamburg, to another Institute, where he introduced writer **Alain Robbe-Grillet** (b. 1922) to striptease clubs, fairgrounds and a hall of mirrors.

Foucault had a fling with a transvestite.

He also took novelist **Pierre Gascar** (b. 1916) to see female mudwrestling in the red-light district. The bars' clientèle called Foucault "*Herr Doktor*".

1960-61 – Rapid Change

Foucault's Dad had died. Foucault used his inheritance to buy a modern flat in rue du Dr Finlay with a view of the Seine.

This was the France of Charles de Gaulle's Fifth Republic. Toll motorways, atom bombs, the new currency, New Wave film, all proclaimed a modern France, but also a troubled one.

Daniel Defert, a student at the École Normale de Saint-Cloud, was introduced to Foucault. They became close partners. Defert was an activist against the war. Foucault avoided the issue and completed research on his *History of Madness* in the archives and libraries of Paris.

From Philosophy to Madness

Between all this, he finished his two theses which he decided to submit at the Sorbonne in Paris.

He first presented a complementary thesis on the Enlightenment philosopher **Immanuel Kant** (1724-1804), in which he used the term "archaeology" for the first time, and which indicated the period of history to which he was constantly to return.

The Enlightenment: the intellectual, philosophical, cultural and scientific spirit of the 18th century. A belief in reason, progress, man's "maturity" and a general rejection of tradition, religion and authority.

Descartes   Newton   Goethe   Kant

It spelt my move beyond science, to the point where philosophy and science had something in common: **reason.**

Jury members then listened to Foucault's major work …

Madness and Civilization (1964)

Madness and Civilization was not a view of the history of madness from a psychiatrist's standpoint.

> This would assume that madness was a constant, negative objective fact – in other words, an account of madness from the point of view of "scientific" reason.

Later Foucault said his object was "knowledge invested in the complex system of institutions". Authorities, their practices and opinions would be studied to show madness not as a scientific or theoretical discourse, but as a regular daily practice.

Folly and Unreason

Foucault instead proposed a close study of madness **itself** (Heideggerian strands here – of its "silence" beyond the language of reason).

"To capture a space, words without a language, the stubborn murmuring of a language which seems to speak quite by itself … breaking down before it has achieved any formulation and passing back without any fuss into the silence from which it was never separated."

We must try to return in history to that "zero point" in the course of madness when it was suddenly separated from reason – both in the **confinement** of the insane and in the conceptual **isolation** of madness from reason, as **unreason.**

blmgkjd... ma sta*to lupam+ bezveze?glb! @neznam!

The Classical Era

Foucault refers to the "classical era" of the 17th and 18th centuries in Europe to show that madness is an object of perception within a "social space" which is structured in different ways throughout history. Madness is an object of perception produced by *social practices*, rather than simply an object of thought or sensibility which could be analyzed.

Foucault contends that before the classical age the relationship of madness to reason was very different.

There are four historical phases and distinct perceptions of madness. Let's look at these.

1. Medieval Madness and Death

In the medieval period – the Middle Ages – man's dispute with madness was a drama in which all the secrets of the world were at stake. The experience of madness was clouded by images of the Fall, God's will, the Beast, the end of time and the world.

Death was the dominant theme. Man's madness was in *not* seeing that death's reign was nigh. It was therefore necessary to bring him back to wisdom with the spectacle of death.

2. Renaissance Folly

Madness comes to the fore in the late 15th century.

Man's life is no longer mad on account of the inevitability of death, but because death lies at the heart of life itself.

The head that will become a skull is already empty.

Folly's Truth

Madness was the "truth" of knowledge, but the sane man's knowledge and learning were an absurd folly. The literary character of the Fool, in his wise idiocy, already knew this.

> In my folly I show how mad reason itself is.

From the 15th century onwards, through literature, philosophy and art, the subject is tackled in different ways. Madness now exists *in man*.
The experience of madness takes the form of **moral satire**, rather than threats of invasion by the madness of the world which haunted painters like **Hieronymous Bosch** (1450-1516). Folly points to the madness and error of reason itself.

"The Ship of Fools" was a symbolic presentation of the banishment and voyage of the mad in search of reason.

3. The Classical Age of Confinement

The classical age (roughly 1650-1800) reduced to **silence** the madness that the Renaissance had given imaginary freedom. It was contained and bound to reason, to morals and rights.

Confinement is the practice which corresponds most exactly to madness experienced as **unreason,** that is, as the empty negativity of reason. By confinement, madness is acknowledged to be *nothing*.

Old, empty leper houses were used for a new purpose – to **confine**. The age of reason banged up the insane as well as the poor. In 1656, a decree founded the Hôpital Général in Paris. One in a hundred Parisians was locked up – the mad with the poor and the criminal.

Bourgeois Morals

In fact, the confinement had more to do with economic problems of unemployment, idleness and begging. A new ethic of work and new ideas of moral obligation were now linked to civil law. Work was redemption. Idleness was rebellion. Beggars were often shot by archers at the city gates ...

Whereas the Renaissance had allowed madness into the light, the classical age saw it as scandal or shame. Families secreted mad uncles and strange cousins in asylums.

But spectacle played its part. At Bethlehem hospital in London, lunatics were displayed to 96,000 people a year. Madness had once been mimed, now it was presented as flesh and blood – no longer a monster inside oneself, but a thing to look at and to contain.

Treated Like Animals

The confinement wasn't inspired by a desire to punish or correct – simply to discipline and sever. So the insane had a beast-like existence behind bars, chained to walls and gnawed by rats.

The madman is *not* a sick man. His animality makes him impervious to cold, hunger and pain. His animal-madness protects him.

The medicine of the period perceived madness as an excessive movement of dangerous passions – too much grief or food led to melancholia and delirium.

Cures for madness were directed at the body of the insane person, as well as his imagination. These were usually conducted *outside* the hospitals.

Music, running, travel, immersion in cold water, purification with cleaning agents and "soapy foods" – and even wounding – alleviated boiling spirits.

Reform, Asylums and Capture of Minds

Late 18th century psychiatric reformers saw punitive measures as ill-treatment. The insane were physically liberated and placed under a moral educational and psychiatric discourse. But, in fact, they were now less free because even their *minds* were subject to treatment.

Reason and unreason are now separate: psychiatric language is installed as a monologue of *reason about madness*.

The mad person is now his own category – a patient – subject to "reasoned" care and **treatment.**

The principle of fear is considered as of great importance in the management of the patient, in reasoning with him and appealing to his sense of self-esteem.

Samuel Tuke (1784-1857)

Philippe Pinel (1745-1826)

Madness was a social failure rather than a Fall. The asylum mirrored the bourgeois authoritarian order!

4. 1900 and Freud the Divine

Personalities like **Sigmund Freud** (1856-1939) silenced condemnation of madness. He abolished **régimes of silence** that reformers had employed. He made the mad *talk*. But he also developed the structure which included the medical personage – him – as omnipotent and quasi-divine.

For Foucault, the only way for madness to live "in itself", outside of authoritarian reason, is through art and philosophy.

The world that thought to measure and justify madness through psychology must justify itself before madness – before the excess of works like those of Artaud, Van Gogh and Nietzsche.

Critical Reception

Foucault's work calls into question the origins of psychology's scientific status, without submitting to the authority of historical sources of information. It doesn't attempt to define madness. It shows ways in which it was experienced, imagined and dispersed – phenomenologically – with some lip-service paid to structural change (economics, society, science).

Some criticized its lack of historical qualities and its distortions.

Not all madness is of artistic interest.

But madness is best heard in literature.

Writer **Maurice Blanchot** (b. 1907)

Anti-Psychiatry

Look at my journal *Les Temps Modernes*: "Foucault sees a history which both produces viable concepts of madness, then as a space which totally misrecognizes madness as an object. That's a contradiction."

Yet he's shaken France's intellectual habits.

Roland Barthes

Jean-Paul Sartre

The book was embraced by anti-psychiatry and the counter-cultural theory of **R.D. Laing** (1927-89) and **David Cooper** (1931-86), and then in *Anti-Oedipus: Capitalism and Schizophrenia* (1972) by **Gilles Deleuze** (b. 1925) and **Félix Guattari** (b. 1930).

Foucault vs. Derrida, 1963

In a lecture, post-structuralist **Jacques Derrida** (b. 1930) deconstructed Foucault's three pages in *Madness and Civilization* which discuss the *Méditations* of **René Descartes** (1596-1650).

Foucault had attempted to write a history of madness itself ...

This is the maddest part of Foucault. How can *he* avoid the violence that the language of reason (order, truth, the system of objectivity and universal rationality) shows to madness?

Foucault has misread Descartes. He assumed the rationalist philosopher had used madness to promote reason, but this is not the case. Reason and madness are less obviously opposed here than Foucault thinks.

Yawn...

Foucault's structuralist totalitarianism here is similar to the violences of the classical age.

CRACK!

The two intellectuals fell out over this.

49

Clermont-Ferrand – Conflict Begins

Foucault had become a respected intellectual. He wrote articles and attended conferences, reviewed literature and spoke on religious deviation. Canguilhem's report and Hyppolite's support led to a job offer from the University of Clermont-Ferrand in 1960. He taught psychology.
When Communist philosopher **Roger Garaudy** (b. 1913) moved there, with the alleged influence of premier **Georges Pompidou** (1911-74), a bitter feud began.

They came to blows.

Language and Literature

Foucault's interest in literature was at its height here, particularly in novels which explored the mad slippage between language, its sense and the worlds it made, such as the crazy *Locus Solus* (1914) by **Raymond Roussel** (1877-1933).

les lettres du blanc sur les bandes du vieux billard (the letters in white around the edges of the old billiard table)

can be changed into

les lettres du blanc sur les bandes du vieux pillard (the white man's letters about the old plunderer's gangs)

The description is not language's faithfulness to its object, but the constantly renewed birth of an infinite relationship between **words and things**.

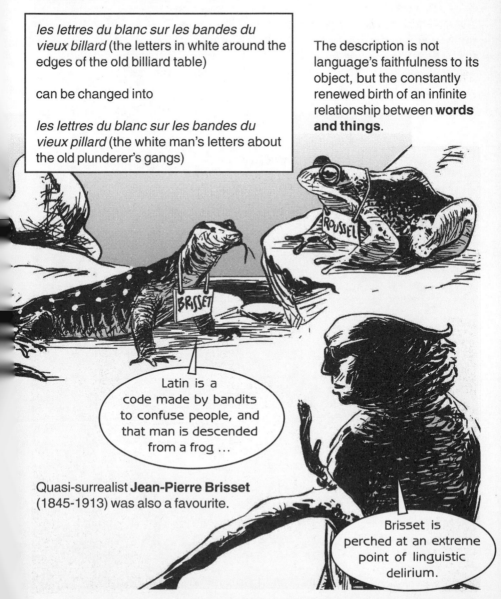

Latin is a code made by bandits to confuse people, and that man is descended from a frog ...

Quasi-surrealist **Jean-Pierre Brisset** (1845-1913) was also a favourite.

Brisset is perched at an extreme point of linguistic delirium.

Medicine and Methodology

In 1963, Foucault published *The Birth of the Clinic: an Archaeology of Medical Perception*, based on his reading of every book of clinical medicine produced between 1790 and 1820. "This book is about space, about language and about death; it is about the act of seeing, the gaze."

Clinical medicine was more than just opinions. It became linked to 19th century **sciences** like biology, physiology and anatomy, as well as **institutions** like hospitals and **practices** such as administrative inquiry. Foucault wanted to account for the **rules** of this knowledge.

I wondered how it was that knowledge could have arisen, changed, developed and offered scientific theory new fields of observations and objects, and how scientific learning had been imported into it.

BIOLOGY
PHYSIOLOGY
ANATOMY
INQUIRY
OBSERV
OBJECTS

The model of sight, seeing and naming is opened in science.

Medical Knowledge Mutates

The practice of medicine is a shaky mixture of rigorous science and uncertain tradition. As a system of knowledge, however, it finds its own coherency. And this knowledge transforms over time – from a language of fantasy and myth …

… to one which assumes objectivity.

Structuralism

This is also a quasi-**structuralist** study of how medical discourses organize themselves in **relation** to different structures – political, social, cultural and economic – and to each other, in order to demonstrate the changes that affected how things were spoken or seen, and what it was possible to see and say in a historical period.

I do **not** attempt to formulate a *truth* or *ground* for medical knowledge, nor do I see medicine as a gradual linear process of improvement or medical enlightenment.

Medicine simply reorganizes disease according to new patterns of syntax – new relationships between language and what it names, in relation to other structural changes in society, its practices and institutions.

Knowledge as Classification

Our perception of the body as the natural "space of the origin and distribution of disease", a space determined by the **anatomical atlas**, is merely one of the various ways in which medicine has formed its "knowledge".

Medicine of Species (1770) classified diseases as **species** with no necessary connection to the body.

Diseases were conceived as transferring to the body when their qualities combine with the patient's temperament.

This was **classificatory** medical thought.

This **spatialization** of illness was conceptual. Disease was ordered hierarchically in families, genera and species in terms of analogy and resemblance. "Catarrh is to the throat what dysentery is to the intestine." The patient was a potential *obstacle* to the perception of the formal class or species.

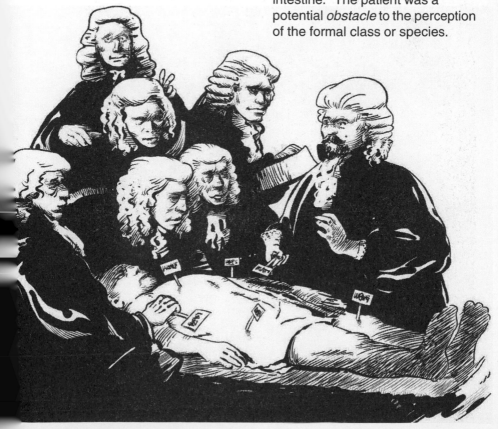

Symptoms

Later, **clinical medicine** (1800s onwards) saw and "thought" diseases as **symptoms** rather than fixed entities or species on a chart. These were in turn interpreted as **signs** of pathological development. Illness was no longer about the distribution of species and their relationships, but was now spatialized on the body as nothing more than a collection of symptoms.

So now clinical language is in complete accord with what it names. Speaking and seeing are one. This is the speaking eye of the clinical doctor.

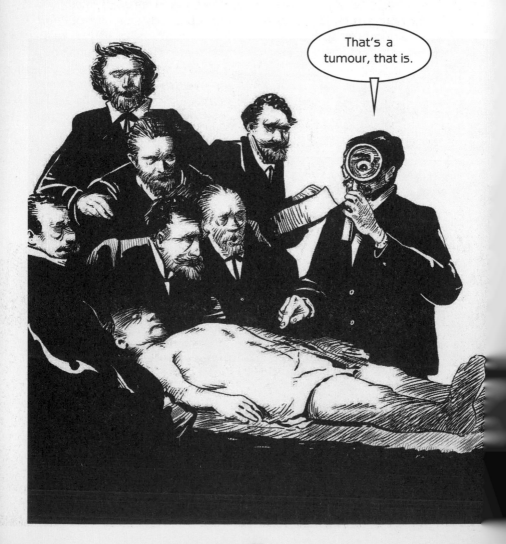

Anatomy – The Technique of the Corpse

Pathological anatomy is developed – or **anatomo-clinical** theory. Disease did not denote species or sets of symptoms, but indicated lesions in specific tissues.

The clinical gaze over the body's surface becomes a gaze **into** the body.

This is the gaze of dissection, which inaugurates the medicine of pathological reactions. The tissues and organs are now the site of the illness. The notion of classes of illness has gone.

Microscopes give a technical dimension to this new gaze.

Man and Death

Death is no longer an absolute fact, cutting off life and the course of disease. Death is now the dominant conceptual principle.

It is not the negative, infinite "night" after the body expires.

Death is a process which can be identified in failing organs and decomposition.

"The medical gaze is no longer that of the medical eye, but the gaze of an eye that has seen death – a great white eye that unties the knot of life." Foucault follows **Georges Bataille** (1887-1962). Certainly Bataille's erotic and death-fixated *Story of the Eye* provided him with the eye as a viable concept.

Barthes Gets Jealous

Foucault's book soon became a cult …

Praise for Foucault's book: "It allowed the profession to see that medicine was not simply a mechanical practice, but also a language which had evolved over time." Dr Bernard Kouchner

Criticism of Foucault's book: "Foucault fails to see beyond his own episteme. He is a product of 20th century French thought which privileges or challenges ocular society – philosophies of visual perception, looking, examining, painting, etc. He should look at his own premises in promoting the eye as dominant principle." Martin Gay, academic

But structuralists claim his links between the social context of the French Revolution, its clinics and the shift in perceptual structures, are oblique …

We've sworn to remain together forever!

Apparently, Barthes fell out with Foucault because he coveted Defert, who was living with Foucault in rue du Dr Finlay.

Nietzsche to the Rescue

Foucault had first read Nietzsche on a beach in Italy with his chum **Maurice Pinguet** in August 1953.

In a July 1964 conference on Nietzsche, Foucault discussed history and **interpretation**, using the "three masters of suspicion": **Friedrich Nietzsche** (1844-1900), **Sigmund Freud** (1856-1939) and **Karl Marx** (1818-83).

After ten years, Foucault is still struggling with philosophy to escape the Hegelian and Marxist idea of history unfolding towards an **absolute** as a resolution of contradictions and conflicts. Who can he turn to?

What interested Foucault in 1964 was the infinite nature of **interpretation** – Marx's interpretations of bourgeois ideological interpretations; Freud's of his patients' interpretations of their neuroses; and Nietzsche's in his claim that philosophy does not find knowledge but imposes endless interpretations. Why was Nietzsche especially helpful to Foucault?

No More Knowledge

For Nietzsche, it was inconceivable to imagine that history will move towards a whole or reveal a total truth.

This presents a radical possibility of a break with Hegelian thought and its contention that history leads us to Absolute and total knowledge. This places reason in doubt!

It could pertain to the fundamental nature of existence that a complete knowledge of truth would destroy one.

Hegel's dialectic – which moves towards completion of knowledge – is undone by Nietzsche.

Words and Things

Foucault's interest in language and interpretation of the world led to his next book, **The Order of Things: An Archaeology of the Human Sciences**, written mostly by mid-1964 and expanded in lectures in Brazil in 1965.

It was the biggest pain in the arse to write.

Foucault's purpose is to look at how man became the object of knowledge in Western culture. He does this by taking three periods in history – the Renaissance, the classical era and the modern era – and unearthing each epoch's respective historical *a priori*.

The latent grid of knowledge which organizes every scientific discourse and defines what can or cannot be thought scientifically – the process of uncovering these levels Foucault calls **archaeology**.

His project is to find the historical and fundamental codes of our culture – our present – not to reveal phenomenological perceptions of it.

Key Term No. 1: Archaeology

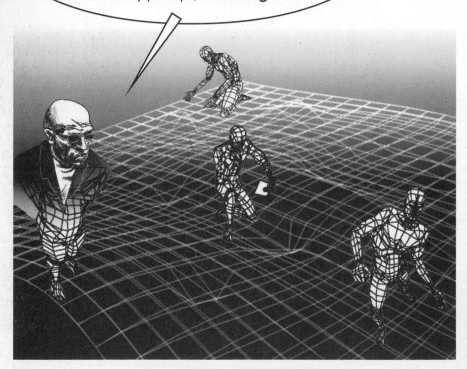

"Archaeology", as the investigation of that which renders necessary a certain form of thought, implies an excavation of unconsciously organized sediments of thought. Unlike a **history of ideas**, it doesn't assume that knowledge accumulates towards any historical conclusion. Archaeology ignores individuals and their histories. It prefers to excavate **impersonal** structures of knowledge.

Archaeology is a task that *doesn't* consist of treating discourse as signs referring to a real content like madness. It treats discourses, such as medicine, as **practices** that form the objects of which they speak.

Key Term No. 2: Episteme

An **episteme** is the "underground" grid or network which allows thought to organize itself. Each historical period has its own episteme. It limits the totality of experience, knowledge and truth, and governs each science in one period.

Foucault has re-jigged Thomas Kuhn's idea of the **paradigm**.

A science becomes normal when scientists agree that their work has identified and solved scientific problems. This agreed-upon achievement model, I call a paradigm or **exemplar**.

The problem with this model, though, is to account for the way in which one scientific episteme **shifted** to another – or how they overlapped. It was never fully solved.

Taxonomy or Classification

Language is central to the book's project. Foucault presents a short story by the Argentinian writer **Jorge Luis Borges** (1899-1986), about a Chinese encyclopaedia.

It divides animals according to an exotic classification ...

The Renaissance Episteme

Words and **things** were united in their **resemblance**. Renaissance man thought in terms of **similitudes**: the theatre *of* life, the mirror *of* nature. There were four ranges of resemblance.

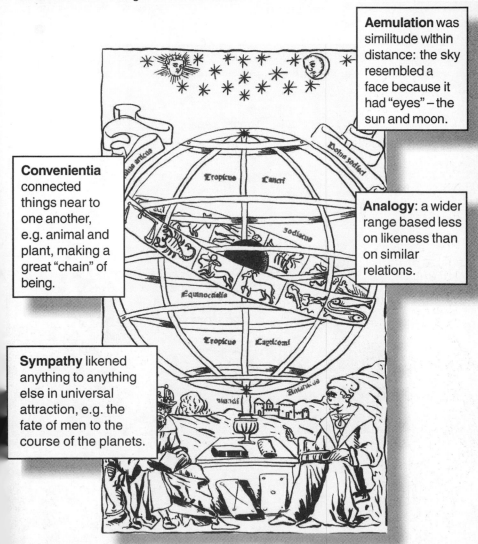

Aemulation was similitude within distance: the sky resembled a face because it had "eyes" – the sun and moon.

Convenientia connected things near to one another, e.g. animal and plant, making a great "chain" of being.

Analogy: a wider range based less on likeness than on similar relations.

Sympathy likened anything to anything else in universal attraction, e.g. the fate of men to the course of the planets.

A "signature" was placed on all things by God to indicate their affinities – but it was hidden, hence the search for arcane knowledge. Knowing was **guessing** and **interpreting**, not observing or demonstrating.

The Classical Episteme

Resemblance collapsed. Discrimination was now used to establish **identities** and **differences**. Knowledge had a new space. It was no longer about guessing, but about order. The classification of stable and separate identities is called **representation**.

Analysis was born, heralded by Don Quixote, the knight created by **Miguel de Cervantes** (1547-1616). Quixote is alienated by analogy in a world of reason based on identities and differences, not signs and similitudes.

I'm using **mathesis** – a universal science of **measurement** and **order** …

And there is also **taxinomia** – a principle of **classification** and ordered **tabulation**.

Knowledge replaced universal resemblance with finite differences. History was arrested and turned into tables …

Western reason had entered the **age of judgement**.

Classical Signs

In the classical period, language is seen as transparent, with no need for hidden or "occult" links. Signs are no longer placed upon things but are now "within" knowledge, signifying certainty and probability. Pictures and words are not bound up with the order of things, but with representation itself. New empirical fields are now established.

general grammar

Words represent thought. Language is asked how it functions as discourse. Renaissance commentary has yielded to classical criticism.

natural history

Animals are now classified as species, rather than by their history in legend or fable.

the analysis of wealth

No longer the Renaissance worries about the "character" of metal in coinage. Now mercantilism treats gold and silver as a means to analyze all other kinds of wealth in a system of exchange.

Representation Without a Subject

Maids of Honour (*Las Meninas*, 1656) by **Diego Velásquez** (1599-1660) is a painting about representation. But of whom? Of nothing but the system of representation.

There is an essential void. The people it resembles (in the mirror, King Philip IV and Queen Mariana) and the spectators who look at them are absent.

Classical representation no longer needs a subject like royalty. It can only be made visible by its invisibility – by appearing in the **mirror of representation**. The true subject is never to be found in the table – or painting – as a historical subject of life, labour and language. The classical episteme did not isolate a specific domain proper to man.

Axiom: In the classical episteme the subject is bound to escape its own representation.

1800s: From Order to History

In the 1800s, a discontinuity spells the end of the classical episteme – a mutation of Order into **History**.

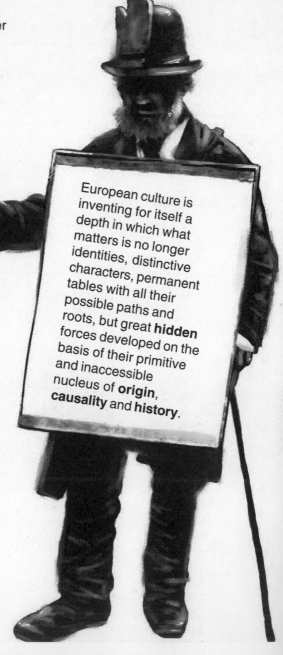

European culture is inventing for itself a depth in which what matters is no longer identities, distinctive characters, permanent tables with all their possible paths and roots, but great **hidden** forces developed on the basis of their primitive and inaccessible nucleus of **origin**, **causality** and **history**.

The **modern** episteme studies man in himself as historical subject. It is *through man* that knowledge is possible in the **empirical** contents of human life: man's body, his social relations, his norms and values.

Deeper forces were substituted for the surface regularities of classical knowledge: dynamic, historical categories of explanation.

Man as Modern Object

Economics

For the economist **David Ricardo** (1772-1823) wealth is now **labour**, measured in time, industrial progress and non-productive labour. **Homo oeconomicus** is the human being who spends, wears out, and wastes his life in evading the imminence of death. He is a **finite** being ...

Biology

In biology, **Georges Cuvier** (1769-1832) becomes concerned with function and disclosing invisibilities through anatomy.

This is the **anthropology** of natural **finitude** – man as his own limit. The anthropological version of knowledge is based on man and not infinity.

Living species "escape" from the teeming confusion of individuals and can be classified only because they are alive and on the basis of what they conceal. Beings are continuous. Life is now seen as the root of all existence, and it has a *biological* history.

Summary

Language is no longer the sovereign means to organize or represent knowledge. It is an object of knowledge like others, to be investigated in the same ways as living things, wealth, value and history.

The question now is not what makes words possible, but are we capable of mastering them? The philosophical struggle now is to make new links between language and *being*.

Man in these modern sciences was now seen in his **actual** existence. If under the classical episteme, man as the central subject of knowledge was missing (as in Velásquez), the modern episteme overdid it by forgetting that man as the centre of thought was simply an epistemic mutation.

Man and His Double

The classical era gave human beings a privileged position in the order of the world. Man was not seen as a finite knowledge outlined by labour, language and body. In the modern episteme, instead, man is both a finite figure and a strange **empirico-transcendental doublet**.

... Knowledge in its historical, social and economic form which "transcends" reference to man himself.

This means that modern thought is unable to avoid the search to separate or reconcile this *double* man: body *vs.* culture, nature *vs.* history, phenomenology (experience) *vs.* Marxism (history).

How Rational are Human Sciences?

But the **human sciences** – psychology, sociology, cultural history etc. – pose a problem in the modern episteme. Can man take himself as an *object of science*? Isn't the idea of man simply a projection of *other* sciences like biology? Aren't *human* sciences too empirical and too changeable to be thought of as anything other than irregular?

Psychoanalysis or ethnology never get close to a general concept of man. They **unmake** man, the dense object of the positive sciences like biology … But this has its good side.

These **counter-sciences** (psychoanalysis, ethnology), which pursue this "Other", keep **self-criticism** of man at maximum power.

The End of Man – Is the Subject Finished?

The last lines of *The Order of Things*: "Before the end of the 18th century, man did not exist. As the archaeology of our thought easily shows, man is an invention of recent date. And one perhaps nearing its end."

Foucault proclaims the eclipse of man as a ground of thought and suggests that knowledge itself may be no more than our persistent self-delusion!

He wrote in 1964 of the death of **homo dialecticus** – man who regains historical truth.

Simone de Beauvoir

J.P. Sartre

Man as an object of knowledge is in difficult circumstances!

But in fact this idea of "historical man" was built on a system of knowledge where the human sciences are no science, and science itself possesses no logical stability, no lasting criteria of truth and validity.

The book became a bestseller – but it disturbed Sartreans, Marxists and Catholic humanists ...

Criticisms

One criticism of Foucault was that he made the break between classical and modern epistemes too stark, too block-like. What about epistemic overlaps or lags? And what about the role of mathematics and hard sciences in history?

Foucault provides bourgeois consciousness with its best alibis. They suppress history, praxis, that is to say commitment, and suppress man.

You are so intent on the progressive aspects of history that you perceive any criticism of it as neo-capitalist!

Cang

And we Catholic humanists think the death of man is hard to stomach!

Marxism exists in 19th century thought in the same way a fish exists in water — it stops breathing anywhere else!

Sartre said that Foucault brought people what they needed — an eclectic synthesis to demonstrate the impossibility of historical reflection.

This is Not a Pipe

Belgian Surrealist artist **René Magritte** (1898-1967) wrote a letter to Foucault, attempting to explain the difference between similitude (of **things**, like the colour of peas) and resemblance (of **thought**, which "resembles" the world it sees).

Foucault in his reply and text of 1973 took as an example and title Magritte's *This is Not a Pipe* (1926) and *The Two Mysteries* (1966). The problem of resemblance – the relation between words and things – is studied in these paintings.

Let's look at their **heterotopic** approach – meaning one **or** other – where the traditional bonds between language and image are disturbed, made different and in tension.

Ceci n'est pas une pipe.

Foucault traces two relevant principles in Western painting which lead from the 15th century to Magritte's work.

Image and Text

In paintings or illustrations, text (words) and images (resemblances) often appear together, but one is always **subordinate** to the other. For example, an illustration can serve a text, or a letter in a *trompe l'oeil* painting might serve the image. There is a **hierarchy** of resembling the world through images and using non-resemblance (representation) through words (they don't look like the world).

Modernists such as **Paul Klee** (1879-1940) tried to get round this **separation** by collapsing resemblance into representation. Klee makes little figures or trees (images) look like signs (words). This is a new space beyond classical hierarchies in painting.

Resemblance was always an **affirmation** of an object. When an image is painted, a statement is assumed. "What you see is that."

Wassily Kandinsky (1866-1944) tried to dissolve representation by painting abstract forms which were affirming that they were "things" – "that's a yellow triangle" – while not representing anything.

Magritte to Warhol

Magritte's work seems to pursue resemblance to its Surrealist limit (a ship will look not just like a ship, but its sails will be painted as waves). But it is totally committed to tearing apart representation (words) and resemblance (images).

Although the pipe resembles a pipe, the statement runs against the identity of the image. Magritte shows the problems of resemblance and representation.

Campbell, Campbell, Campbell, Campbell...

Ask yourself:
What is here "*not* a pipe"? The image, the text, the word "This"? And both image and text are painted in the same medium ... so they are similar, yet different. The more text and image try to converge, the less sense there is!

Magritte's painting undermines representation, or the relation of signs to world, but it also refuses to close the gap between image and word. Only similitudes remain – a series of visual and linguistic signs without external reference. With the soup cans of **Andy Warhol** (1928-87), similitude is multiplied endlessly in the image.

Tunisia! 1966

Foucault took a post in the University of Tunis in Morocco. The relaxed lifestyle suited him – good food, cannabis and handsome young men. He lived in Sidi Bou Saïd – then a colony of arty French expatriates – overlooking the sea. Defert visited him often.

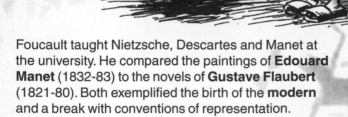

Foucault moved to a converted stable, and slept on a mat on a raised platform. The locals thought this philosopher was a necromancer!

Foucault taught Nietzsche, Descartes and Manet at the university. He compared the paintings of **Edouard Manet** (1832-83) to the novels of **Gustave Flaubert** (1821-80). Both exemplified the birth of the **modern** and a break with conventions of representation.

In Manet's work, the painted surface does not mask its materiality. It draws attention to its "paintedness".

Le Bar des Folies-Bergère is one example.

Fights

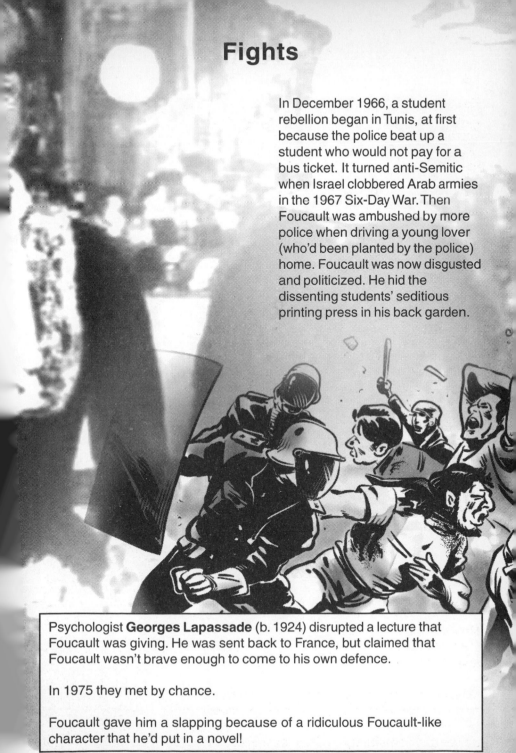

In December 1966, a student rebellion began in Tunis, at first because the police beat up a student who would not pay for a bus ticket. It turned anti-Semitic when Israel clobbered Arab armies in the 1967 Six-Day War. Then Foucault was ambushed by more police when driving a young lover (who'd been planted by the police) home. Foucault was now disgusted and politicized. He hid the dissenting students' seditious printing press in his back garden.

Psychologist **Georges Lapassade** (b. 1924) disrupted a lecture that Foucault was giving. He was sent back to France, but claimed that Foucault wasn't brave enough to come to his own defence.

In 1975 they met by chance.

Foucault gave him a slapping because of a ridiculous Foucault-like character that he'd put in a novel!

Structural Space

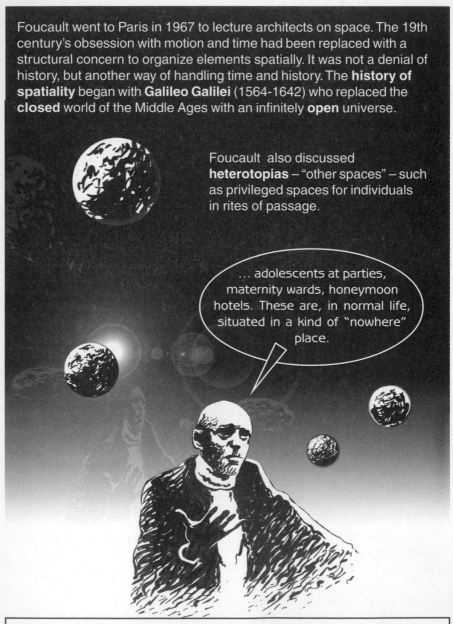

Foucault went to Paris in 1967 to lecture architects on space. The 19th century's obsession with motion and time had been replaced with a structural concern to organize elements spatially. It was not a denial of history, but another way of handling time and history. The **history of spatiality** began with **Galileo Galilei** (1564-1642) who replaced the **closed** world of the Middle Ages with an infinitely **open** universe.

Foucault also discussed **heterotopias** – "other spaces" – such as privileged spaces for individuals in rites of passage.

... adolescents at parties, maternity wards, honeymoon hotels. These are, in normal life, situated in a kind of "nowhere" place.

His point was made later when he said, "Space is fundamental in any exercise of power."

The Archaeology of Knowledge (1969)

This book is both a methodological inquiry into knowledge, history and discourse and a self-criticism. In *Madness and Civilization* and *The Birth of the Clinic*, Foucault said he'd given too much credit to the experience of madness in itself. Its history was too subject-centred – rooted in a philosophy of consciousness.

This new book provided the syntheses. Knowledge was an area between opinion and scientific knowledge, and it was embodied not only in theoretical texts or experimental instruments, but in a whole body of practices and institutions.

He looked at the longer-term stable periods *beneath* historical events and personalities ...

... such as we did in the **Annales** school of history.

... and contrasted that with Gaston Bachelard's epistemological ruptures and Canguilhem's transformations ...

... discontinuous and displaced history.

History for me was now both depersonalized and formed of complex relations and rules – discursive formations.

Discourse

Foucault drops epistemes as the dominant principle in history and asserts **discourse**.

Discourses are not linguistics systems or just texts – they are **practices**, like the scientific discourse of psychoanalysis and its institutional, philosophical and scientific levels.

By analyzing **statements** – single units which constitute a discursive formation – we can see their constraints and where they situate the speaker.

In this case, the patient and analyst.

Any institution implies the existence of statements in charters, contracts, registrations, etc.

Rules of Discourse

There are three rules of forming discourse. Discourse requires …

Surfaces of emergence: social and cultural areas through which discourse appears, e.g. the family, work group or religious community.
Authorities of delimitation: institutions with knowledge and authority, like the law or the medical profession.
Grids of specification: a system by which different kinds of madness, say, can be related to each other in psychiatric discourse.

Studying Discourse

Foucault states that all history is a **document** of the past – the traces it leaves in our **present** through books, accounts, acts, buildings, customs.

But we should treat these documents like monuments – not for their reference to historical validity, but for themselves.

Documents should not be studied in order to determine their historical accuracy. This would be to reconstitute the "truth" of history.

Discourse Creates its Object

When medical, legal and judicial discourses refer to madness, they never refer to a fixed object or experience, and they don't treat it as the same object. Yet there may be regularities between these discourses.

Links made by psychiatric discourse between criminal and pathological behaviour don't imply a scientific and historical "discovery" of "mad criminals" or identify a social context for this behaviour ...

Criminal behaviour can give rise to whole series of objects of knowledge (criminal character, hereditary and environmental factors) only because a set of **rules** and **conditions** were established between **institutions**, **economic and social practices** and **patterns of behaviour**. These do not add up to criminality, but their relations and differences allow us to say certain things about criminality as discourse.

Foucault and Althusser ...

Foucault's idea of the **statement** corresponds to the term **ideology**, as used by the Marxist philosopher **Louis Althusser** (1918-90).

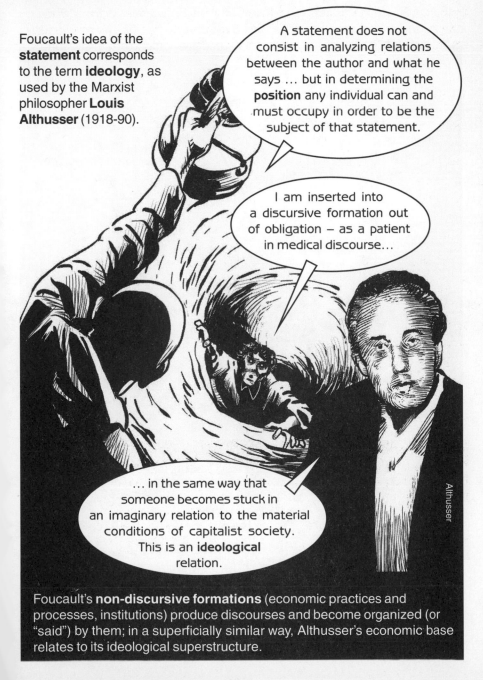

A statement does not consist in analyzing relations between the author and what he says ... but in determining the **position** any individual can and must occupy in order to be the subject of that statement.

I am inserted into a discursive formation out of obligation – as a patient in medical discourse...

... in the same way that someone becomes stuck in an imaginary relation to the material conditions of capitalist society. This is an **ideological** relation.

Althusser

Foucault's **non-discursive formations** (economic practices and processes, institutions) produce discourses and become organized (or "said") by them; in a superficially similar way, Althusser's economic base relates to its ideological superstructure.

Against Structuralism

Although Foucault was seen as a member of the Structuralist Gang of Four, alongside Barthes, Lacan and **Claude Lévi-Strauss** (b. 1908), he wasn't really a structuralist. There was too much history and phenomenology in his work.

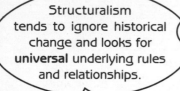

Structuralism tends to ignore historical change and looks for **universal** underlying rules and relationships.

In language or myth, for example.

Permanent structures into which individuals are born.

Structuralism is ultimately rejected by Foucault as too monolithic, too static and too inflexible to transformations.

I differ from those who are called "structuralist" in that I am not greatly interested in the formal possibilities presented by a system such as language ... this particular controversy is now acted out only by mimes and tumblers. My archaeology **historicizes** meaning.

Reception of Archaeology

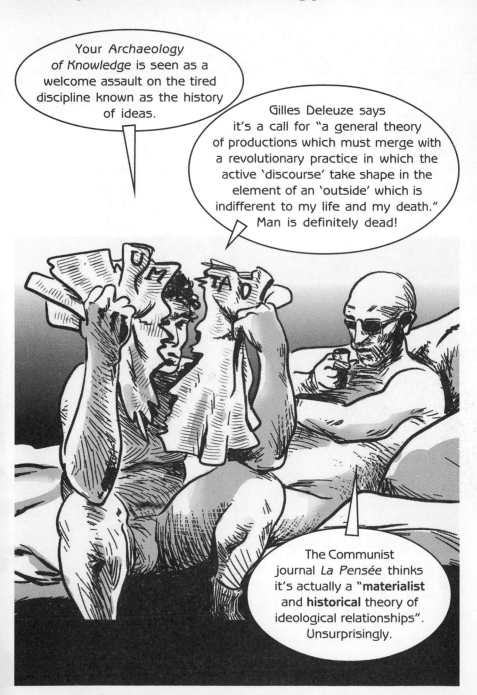

1968 – Paris in Turmoil

When Foucault returned to Paris in late 1968, he was bald. He also wore a roll-neck sweater to save on ironing.

Shaving his head put off age, and it looked hard – like gay criminal Jean Genet.

WELCOME TO PARIS!

He returned to an unstable society. The Situationists, a band of radical subversives who demanded revolution in everyday life, had turned Paris into turmoil.

Georges Pompidou's reinstatement as premier and police brutality didn't help matters. Paris had seen demos, violence and barricades on 6 May.

Foucault took a post at the University of Nanterre, but bored with psychology, he resigned after two weeks and moved to teach philosophy at the University of Vincennes.

Vincennes – on Show

This new university was run on "participation" – everyone had a say. But the French Communist Party saw this as a trap: "a resurrection of the old liberal ideology. It consists of a denial of the reality of class antagonisms and of the assertion that the citizens of a nation – or all members of a company – have an equal interest in its prosperity."

It was a well-equipped college and the first to teach psychoanalysis proper. Jacques Lacan visited and observed that the Pompidou régime was putting the university on display. The government was giving the lefties a playground to fight over. Students baited him.

January 1969: Vincennes Aggro

When students at the Lycée Saint-Louis were prevented by the police from watching films about May 1968, Vincennes students, joined by Defert and Foucault (dressed in a fetching corduroy suit) erected barricades in support and threw rocks.

When the police stormed the University, Foucault was arrested.

Excellent for his credibility – but he suffered the effects of tear gas!

Vincennes became notorious: vandalism, graffiti, a market in stolen books, drugs and a heavy police presence. Groups like the Gauche Prolétarienne wanted the university to function on the basis of worse is better. Revolutionary Maoists spat on Communist Party students.

In this ultra-leftist climate, Communism was seen as a bourgeois front – and I was also an enemy!

Hyppolite Expires

Jean Hyppolite died in October 1968. His chair at the Collège de France was now vacant. Foucault was on the list of applicants. He had to submit his teaching project.

I want to examine what constitutes a science when one wants to analyze it not in transcendental terms but in terms of history, to determine how knowledge recorded the phenomena that until then were external to it.

He was successful and formally became professor of the "history of systems of thought" at the Collège in April 1970.

His inaugural lecture in December spelt a change in direction. "The Discourse on Language" outlined his new thoughts…

The Will to Truth

"In every society, the production of discourse is at once controlled, selected, organized and redistributed according to a certain number of procedures whose role is to avert its powers and its dangers."

This was a **history of the present** and of current societies' respect for and organization of discourse – but this hid a fear of **disorderly discourse**. Society exercises constraint on "dangerous" discourse by excluding, prohibiting, dividing, disciplining and rejecting it.

Discourse is a **will to truth** – pushing away everything it can't assimilate. Nietzsche exposed this.

Knowledge is the result of conflicting desires, characterized by the will to dominate or appropriate. It is unstable and violent.

New Term: Genealogy

Genealogy describes Foucault's attempt to reveal discourse at the moment it appears in history as a system of constraint. Genealogy compels Foucault to analyze literary, biological, medical, religious and ethical bodies of knowledge, and how such "knowledges" might, for example, relate to the discourse on heredity or sexuality. He is led to study the effects of discourses claiming to be scientific – psychiatry, sociology, medicine – on practices such as the penal system, as they first appear.

Genealogy allows for historical change, is not bothered with finding a truth to history or describing neutral, archaeological structures of knowledge, but is interested in history as **will to power.**

Foucault's two-hour lectures at the Collège were always overcrowded. He felt lonely on the lecture stage, surrounded by so many mikes linked up to tape-recorders, even with a troop of admiring young men curled around his feet.

Genealogy Against History

An essay in honour of Hyppolite, entitled **Nietzsche, Genealogy, History**
(1971) indicated the relationship of genealogy to history and philosophy. The
reference to Nietzsche's own *Genealogy of Morals* (1887) is obvious.
Foucault states: "The point is to make such use of history as to free it
forever from the model, which is both metaphysical and anthropological, of
memory. The point is to turn history into a counter-memory."

What is an Author?

Everything is now a mask.

In a lecture entitled "What is an Author?" (1969), Foucault examined the status of the author and his relation to texts. All the conventions we use to "summon" the founding subject of the author are in doubt …

For instance, the author's **name** is not so much about defining his identity, but is part of a discourse of the "author function" – involving appropriation, ownership and a corresponding will to authenticate or get back to the author's **motives**.

Like Nietzsche's body of work. What defines it – just his books?

That's the author function acting to contain his identity. Shouldn't we include his notes, drafts – and even laundry lists?

What difference does it make who is speaking?

"The author does not precede the works; he is a certain functional principle by which, in our culture, one limits, excludes, chooses and impedes the free circulation of fiction."

Tokyo 1970

Foucault visited Japan before taking his post at the Collège. At Tokyo University he replied to Derrida's criticisms of *Madness and Civilization*, and attacked his **deconstructionism** – a strategy of close reading of texts to reveal their contradictions and assumptions.

Derrida reduces discursive practices to textual traces. If there is nothing outside the text, this is a pedagogy – which gives to the voice of the master the limitless sovereignty which allows it to restate the text indefinitely.

This pedagogy teaches the pupil that there is nothing outside the text.

Derrida has misread Descartes' discourse on madness and failed to compare the French and Latin versions of the *Méditations*.

Moving House

Foucault and Defert had moved to a bright eighth-floor flat in a modern block on rue de Vaugirard. They lined the living room with books, grew cannabis amongst the petunias, and entertained characters like **Jean Genet** (b. 1910) and the lovely actress, **Julie Christie** (b. 1940). They had nice views from the terrace, where Foucault enjoyed staring at a young man who appeared each morning in an apartment opposite.

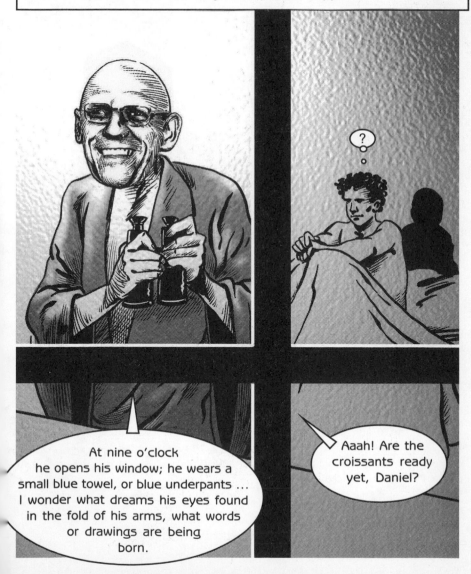

At nine o'clock he opens his window; he wears a small blue towel, or blue underpants ... I wonder what dreams his eyes found in the fold of his arms, what words or drawings are being born.

Aaah! Are the croissants ready yet, Daniel?

Foucault Against Chomsky

On a TV show in Amsterdam, 1971, the rationalist linguist **Noam Chomsky** (b. 1928) sparred with Foucault on the subject of modern power and justice.

Where's the make-up room?

There *is* human nature. This allows us to have a secure scientific understanding. There are innate principles which allow humans to guide our social and intellectual behaviour. I'm looking for a Cartesian and rational mathematical theory of the mind.

Foucault here has a notion of a **specific intellectual** who would provide critical knowledge without posing as a master of truth and justice.

Political Engagement

In December 1971, Foucault helped to found the GIP (*Groupe d'information sur les prisons*). The intellectual was now active!

None of us can be sure of avoiding prison. Police control over our day-to-day lives is becoming tighter: in the streets and on the roads; over foreigners and young people. It is once more an offence to express an opinion.

They tell us prisons are over-populated. But what if it were the population that were being over-imprisoned?

The purpose of the GIP was to gather and disseminate information about the prison system – not to reform it but to expose it via questionnaires sent to prisoners and their families.

All this against a background of prison riots, hunger strikes by GIP prisoners and an oppressive prison régime!

"The guillotine was merely the visible symbol of a system governed by death."

Political Allegiances

Foucault was now acting in support of Maoists, without sharing their belief in "cultural revolution" and a scenario of "imminent civil war".

Some members of the GIP saw the prisoners as an ersatz proletariat. Foucault sometimes described criminality – including shoplifting – as a form of political revolt.

The GIP raided a luxury delicatessen and gave the food to immigrants in the poorer suburbs.

The GIP's first pamphlet attacked power's oppressive disguises: justice, technology, knowledge and objectivity. It argued that the "exploited class" can recognize its oppression and resist it, without needing intellectuals. But by now, other classes were involved: social workers, lawyers and journalists were joining the protests.

Attica

In April 1972, Foucault visited Attica Prison in the USA.

"A phony fortress like Disneyland, observation posts disguised as medieval towers … and behind this rather ridiculous scenery which dwarfs everything else, you discover that it's an immense machine … for elimination."

This experience would have important effects on his next book. Back in Paris, the GIP published "Prison Suicides" (1973), which showed that 72 prisoners – a quarter of them immigrants – had killed themselves in 1972.

The GIP was eclipsed by its success. As the prisoners became organized, the role of the GIP and the Left in general declined by 1973.

The Miner's Murdered Daughter

The notion of "people's justice" – where a public court would put the "system" on trial – had become a worry to Foucault.

The murder in 1972 of 16-year-old girl in the mining town of Bruay-en-Artois led to the population stoning suspect Pierre Leroy's fiancée's house.

The GIP became involved. Jean-Paul Sartre turned up and made a speech – as usual.

Leroy was released without charge.

Immigrants Killed

In November 1972, falsely-arrested Mohammed Diab was shot in a Versailles police station by a policeman who insisted he acted in self-defence – and that he just happened to be carrying a machine-gun at the time.

A protest march was planned in the Paris district where 250 peaceful Algerian demonstrators had been murdered by police in 1961. Their corpses had floated in the Seine.

The meeting exploded into violence. The police charged, but only succeeded in injuring children queuing to watch *101 Dalmatians*.

Foucault and the writer **François Mauriac** were arrested and thrown into a van.

Foucault's friend, the writer and artist **Pierre Klossowski** (b. 1905) suggested a way to stop the police. Simply line up 30 gorgeous men armed with sticks, and their beauty would stop the CRS in its tracks!

Gay Action

Foucault was keen to introduce homosexual issues to the *gauchisme* (leftism) which had hitherto ignored them. In early 1971, the FHAR (*Front Homosexuel d'Action Révolutionnaire*) was founded. Their article read:

YES!
We've been buggered by Arabs; we're proud of it and WE'LL DO IT AGAIN

I went to some meetings, but suspected the FHAR might lead to ghettoization. I think the label "gay" can be as oppressive as any other.

I, Pierre Rivière

Foucault's research project on Pierre Rivière in 1973 consolidated his attempts to see crime as discourse. The unknown 19th-century murderer had slit the throats of his mother, brother and sister. After his arrest he wrote an explanation of the crime for the judge and doctors...

The issue – was he insane? If so, what relation did this lucid text have to his madness?

> The act of killing and the act of writing, the deeds performed and the things recounted, were interwoven like elements of the same nature.

Rivière was **trapped in a discourse beyond him**. He was found guilty, and sent down for life. He killed himself in prison in 1840.

> Yes, but what would it be like *not* to be trapped in discourse?

Critic

...ving slaughtered my mother, my sister and my brother...

I Pierre Rivière

Discipline and Punish

Foucault's lectures of 1972-3 in France and Brazil included an examination of punitive society and judicial power. In 1975, his research led to the publication of *Discipline and Punish – The Birth of the Prison*.

The book is a genealogy of the soul and body in the political, judicial and scientific fields, particularly in relation to punishment, and above all to power over and within **the body**.

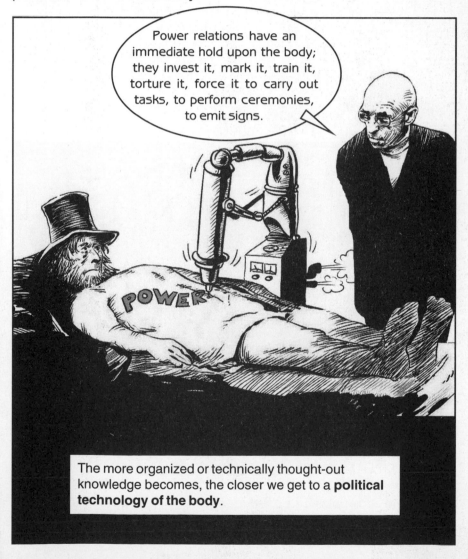

Power relations have an immediate hold upon the body; they invest it, mark it, train it, torture it, force it to carry out tasks, to perform ceremonies, to emit signs.

The more organized or technically thought-out knowledge becomes, the closer we get to a **political technology of the body**.

Micro-physics

Foucault not only studies institutions like the prison, factory, hospital and school, or simply judicial or educational discourses, but also **strategies** of power which bodies *themselves* adopt in relation to institutions.

Foucault calls this dense web of power relations the **micro-physics of power**.

This power is not exercised simply as an obligation or a prohibition on those who "do not have it". It *invests* them, is transmitted by them and through them. It places pressure upon them, and they resist the grip it has on them.

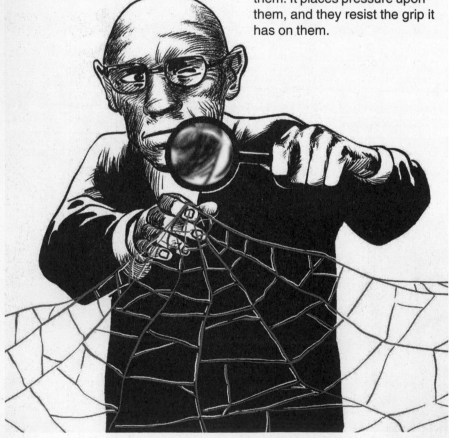

Punishment or discipline has *positive* as well as negative effects on the body – and punishment has a complex social function. Power would be a poor thing if all it did was **oppress**.

From Torture as Spectacle

Foucault charts the shift in punishment from the spectacle of public torture before the 1800s to obsessive over-regulation in prisons (and elsewhere) by the 1830s.

On 2 March 1757, Damiens the regicide was burned with sulphur, his flesh removed with pincers, his wounds covered in boiling liquid, and his limbs harnessed to four horses, stretched, hacked and pulled off. Then the rest of him was chucked on a bonfire – and all in front of the public!

Saving the Soul

But the body as the major target of the State or Monarchy's revenge soon disappeared. The publicity shifted to the trial and the sentence. Physical pain was no longer the prime element of the punishment. Hanging or the guillotine was quick, the condemned man was drugged. Why?

Punishment, by 1760, "struck" the soul. This was nothing to do with kindness, but a new conception of the object, "crime", which involved confronting passions, instincts, drives, effects of environment and heredity.

Now the court judges *itself* in its ability to supervise the criminal with confinement, treatment or correction.

Knowledge of the offence, knowledge of the offender, knowledge of the law; these three conditions made it possible to ground a judgement in truth.

The question now is not "did he do it?" but "what is this act that he has done – what is its cause?"

Bourgeois Methods

In the late 18th century, an organized police apparatus, statistical information on the population, an increase in wealth, and moral value imposed on property relations placed everyday behaviour under **surveillance**. Thieving was not anti-authoritarian but anti-social. The **punitive city** and **coercive institution** were now in place.

Carceral society was born. The object of the 18th-century reforms was not to punish less but to punish or correct better – everywhere!

Rules and Regulations

Crime was now coded, and the power to punish comprised rule-bound **signs**. The new economy and technology together generated what Foucault calls a **semio-technique** based on six rules.

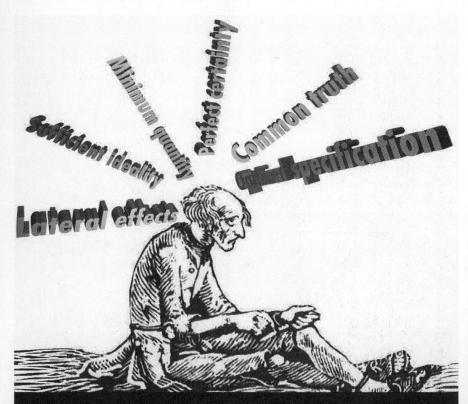

Minimum quantity: punishment must outweigh the advantages of committing a crime.

Sufficient ideality: the idea of pain or representation of punishment should disturb potential criminals.

Lateral effects: the punishment should affect others, making them scared to commit a crime!

Perfect certainty: punishment will inevitably follow the crime.

Common truth: evidence must be weighed according to common standards of proof.

Optimal specification: crimes are codified as classifications and species that *individualize* the criminal by taking into account his wealth, wickedness, etc.

Docile Bodies

And the **prison system** arrives, part of a **disciplinary society**! Punishment followed new rules and resulted in detention, work (morally worthy activity, but also a source of cheap labour) and a régime of cleaning and praying. This was moral reform. "Modern man is born of regulations." The body is now docile – subject to improvement and usefulness. Disciplines are enforced everywhere.

The body becomes a mechanics of power. Soldiers are now trained to march. Factory workers now have posts, skills and timetables. Schoolkids have to sit and write properly.

In all areas, insolence, lateness, laziness, dirtiness and impurity are punished.

117

Bentham's Panopticon

Surveillance and observation are now everywhere, all the time. The Panopticon, designed by Utilitarian philosopher **Jeremy Bentham** (1748-1832), is a tower from which warder, doctor, teacher or foreman can spy on and penetrate behaviour. It locates bodies in space, in relation to each other. The subjects under surveillance never know quite when they are being watched, and so effectively police themselves.

Why do Prisons Fail?

It's obvious that detention and prison "reformation" don't reduce delinquency or crime. Governments therefore conclude that they must punish more harshly or reform better. Foucault turns the question around: "What is served by the failure of prison?" He sees it in terms of delinquency – the system **needs** them.

Police surveillance provides the prison with offenders, whom the prison transforms into delinquents. They become the target of the police, which regularly sends back a certain number of them to prison.

Criticism: Foucault loads the question in order to arrive at his answer. It's a lazy argument.

Power/Knowledge

Prisons are major industries of **power/knowledge**.

Carceral society and its "sciences", such as psychiatry, criminology, psychology and even sociology, ensure that the judges of normality are everywhere. "The carceral network constituted one of the armatures of this power/knowledge that has made the human sciences historically possible. Knowable man (soul, individuality, consciousness, conduct, etc.) is the object/effect of this analytical investment, of this **domination/observation**."

No power is exercised without the extraction, appropriation, distribution or retention of **knowledge.** At this level, we do not have knowledge on the one hand and society on the other, or science and state; we have the basic forms of "power/knowledge".

"Do not demand of politics that it restore the 'rights' of the individual, as philosophy has defined them. The individual is the product of power. What is needed is to 'de-individualize' by means of multiplication and displacement, diverse combinations. Do not become enamoured of power."

Compliments and Criticisms

Discipline and Punish attracted great attention. Most reviews were favourable. "This book will send shock waves through the prison system. It will shake our faith in **ethics**."

Gilles Deleuze said:
"... a very different picture, with different characters and processes, to that which traditional history, even if it is Marxist, has accustomed us."

Foucault has simply given us the reverse of the Enlightenment path to freedom: dystopian unfreedom.

Clifford Geertz

J.G. Merquior:
"Foucault got many facts wrong. He omits the role of the French Revolution in the subsequent replacement of the public guillotine with incarceration. He overplays Enlightenment as a crippling disciplinary drive and he doesn't allow for human agency in his history – so he ends up with conspiracy theory."

Spanish Bio-Fascism

In September 1975, ten freedom fighters from the Basque ETA and the anti-fascist front FRAP were to be garrotted by Franco's régime. Two of the condemned were pregnant.

Foucault flew to Madrid with Yves Montand and others, but was prevented from speaking to the press. The police returned them to a plane of Japanese tourists. Franco generously allowed five militants to be shot rather than garrotted.

The gay dictator died 20 November 1975, having been kept alive for years by his doctors. This was a miniature version of Foucault's **bio-power** – life calculated technically in terms of population, health, national interests, etc.

The man who had the power of life and death over hundreds of thousands of people did not even notice that he was already dead.

1976, Sexuality as History

Foucault's constantly reworked and unfinished project was published. *The History of Sexuality* is an attempt to understand the experience of sexuality in modern Western culture – the birth and growth of "sex" and "sexuality" as historically given objects.

The self-awareness of the individual as the subject of a sexuality. The project required historical inquiry into sexuality, pleasure and friendship in the Ancient, Christian and Modern Worlds. The first of three volumes, *The History of Sexuality: An Introduction*, opened with a bombshell.

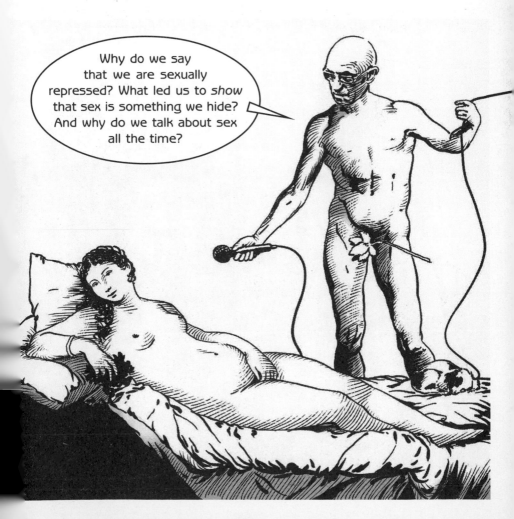

Why do we say that we are sexually repressed? What led us to *show* that sex is something we hide? And why do we talk about sex all the time?

Sex and Power

Since the Renaissance, Western culture began to develop new, powerful techniques for internalizing social norms related to morals and, in particular, to sexual behaviour: a reinforcement of **confession** as a main ritual of truth-production.

The Confessional Animal

Human sciences like psychology, medicine and demography seized on the body as an object of social concern and governmental manipulation. This was **governmentality** at large!

Sex-truth!

The Repressive Hypothesis

Was there ever a **repression** or **censorship** on sex? Foucault says there was rather an **apparatus** for producing greater quantities of discourses on sex. Foucault's point is not whether one says yes or no to sex, but to account for the fact that it is talked about at all.

Foucault is not denying that sex has been prohibited, but he is claiming that repression is a factor which brings **sex into discourse**. In other words, we *talk* about repression – and sex.

Over the last three centuries, we have witnessed a **discursive explosion** – sex being made to speak: the **incitement to discourse**.

From the Catholic confessions to Ricki Lake's chat shows, meticulous rules of self-examination ensure that the vaguest sexual thoughts must be brought to light and tracked down.

Administering Sex

Sex by the 18th century became something administered rather than just judged. The **policing** of sex was linked to the emergent idea of population management. Sexual conduct was an economic and political problem. Debauched rich people were no good to the country.

And now children had a **sexuality**, expressed and organized by school architecture, the layout of dormitories and the introduction of disciplined physical and spiritual education to keep their minds off sex.

The discourse of sexuality was fragmentary yet ubiquitous: demography, biology, medicine, psychiatry, psychology, ethics and pedagogy ...

The Perverse Implantation

The *dispositif* (apparatus) of sexuality refers to the relevant heterogeneous body of discourses, philanthropic propositions, institutions, laws and scientific statements. The *dispositif* itself is the network that binds them together.

In the 19th century, legal sanctions against minor perversions and sexual deviancy became associated with **mental illness**.

Christian morals and civil law performed this **perverse implantation**. The **deployment** of normal and pathological sexuality had four objects: the hysterical woman, the masturbating child, the Malthusian couple (population growth), and the perverse adult.

Homospecies and the Etymology of Sex

"Aberrations" like masturbation, homosexuality and sodomy are incorporated by the medico-sexual régime – its focus being the bourgeois family milieu.

Previously, homosexuality had just been a forbidden act. Now the homosexual was a personage, with a case history, a childhood, and perhaps a mysterious physiology. He was now a **species**.

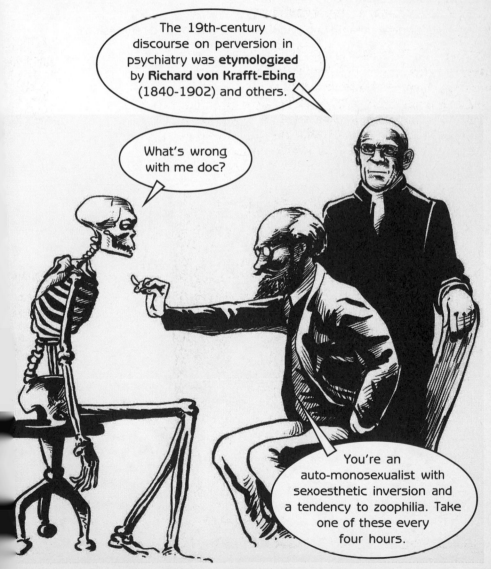

The 19th-century discourse on perversion in psychiatry was **etymologized** by **Richard von Krafft-Ebing** (1840-1902) and others.

What's wrong with me doc?

You're an auto-monosexualist with sexoesthetic inversion and a tendency to zoophilia. Take one of these every four hours.

20th Century: Reveal All!

Taboos and repressions were gradually lifted. Sex in the 20th century was re-conceived as liberation. Yet, at another level, we are still **inciting** sex to discourse. "People will be surprised at the eagerness with which we went about pretending to rouse from its slumber a sexuality which everything – our discourses, our customs, our institutions, our regulations, our knowledges – was busy producing in the light of day and broadcasting to noisy accompaniment."

Is Madonna the tail-end pop discourse of liberation and repression?

Reception to Foucault's book was muted.

Criticism: He makes too much of the confessional link to the Church. Sexuality is reduced to religious practice.

The Baudrillard Incident

Jean Baudrillard (b. 1929), the transgressive French anti-theorist, published a paper, dangerously entitled "Forget Foucault" (1977).

Foucault's discourse is a mirror of the power it describes.

Foucault places too much emphasis on power as the full and ultimate principle, even at its micro-levels. He simply reproduces its effects. But power is challenged by seduction – which can make it disappear!

My seduction theory is more subtle. It can make power collapse by using appearances to seduce.

Foucault blew his top. The master's intellect had been impugned!

Baudrillard was banned!

But Baudrillard had done Foucault a favour. By "forgetting" him, he had shown how the sycophants and hangers-on were turning Foucault into a senseless caricature!

131

Foucault's America

Foucault was invited to the University of Berkeley, California, in 1975. Foucault loved California. He lectured on child sexuality, repression and "abnormal" practices – sketching out his last major work. But there were pleasures to be had beyond the lecture theatre. He found time to relax in the desert on acid and extend his use of drugs – an expression of pleasure **beyond** sex.

LSD reveals this whole univocal and a-categorical mass to be rainbow-coloured, mobile, asymmetrical, decentred, spiraloid and resonating. Far out!

He was familiar with opium, cocaine, poppers and LSD. One trip was so rough he nearly entered a New York police station to ask for valium – and he was knocked down by a car while on opium. "Cocaine de-anatomizes the sexual localization of pleasure – which is now everywhere in the body."

Sado-Masochism: Beyond Desire

Bath-houses, leather and sado-masochism – Foucault indulged himself in New York and San Francisco. He later said that bath-houses with 800 blokes didn't have an equivalent in the heterosexual community. Tough on heterosexuals, he thought.

Discussing homosexual practice in subsequent interviews, Foucault said S & M was not an aggressive practice, but created new pleasures – like golden showers, scatology and fistfucking.

Pleasure is beyond desire, because it escapes the medical and naturalistic notions associated with the latter, and its label of "abnormal".

He visited the Mineshaft in New York's meatpacking district to conduct his research. "S & M is the eroticization of power. Ouch – nice!"

Blindspots

Foucault – **always ambivalent about the state and its power** – was invited by a government commission to advise on censorship and sexuality. In a series of subsequent discussions, the questions of rape and child abuse were posed. Feminists agreed with Foucault that rape was a matter of violence rather than sexuality.

But we can't deal with your claim that our demand for more serious punishment for rapists is phallocentric.

You are implying that certain parts of the body (the sexual parts) are more important than others.

Rape is not the same as a blow in the face and isn't just about physical violence!

Child Abuse – or Consent?

Foucault was more circumspect about the question of child abuse and the sexual, psychological and legal apparatus that controlled it. With teenagers at least, Foucault claimed that they could seduce adults.

And although the current climate was against adult-child relationships, he was unsure about whether the law should intervene. His position, at best, was uncertain.

Zen Techniques

Foucault went to Japan again in April 1978 – he loved the country, and sported a kimono in his Paris flat. He tried a stint at being a monk. "What is most interesting to me is life in a Zen temple itself."

In keeping with his ongoing project of techniques of the self, he was interested in the contrast between Christian spirituality which attempts to inquire into the individual soul – "tell me who you are" – and Zen mysticism – "I'm nobody, going nowhere" – where techniques obliterate the individual. His Zen master taught him how to sit and breathe.

He spoke in Tokyo on power and philosophy.

Philosophy could become a **counter-power** if the philosopher abandoned his prophetic role and began to think about **specific** political struggles rather than universal ones.

To relax he went to tiny gay clubs in Tokyo which only held about six people.

The Iran Mistake

Foucault's strategic politics found an outlet with the Iran crisis. Black Friday – 8 September 1978 – had seen the Shah's army kill 4,000 people in a crowd. Foucault adopted a journalistic role and flew in to Teheran. "Intellectuals will work together with journalists at the point where ideas and events intersect."

He thought a military coup followed by a dictatorship would not happen because Islam strongly opposed state power.

An Islamic government cannot restrict people's rights because it is bound by religious duty. The people will know what is right.

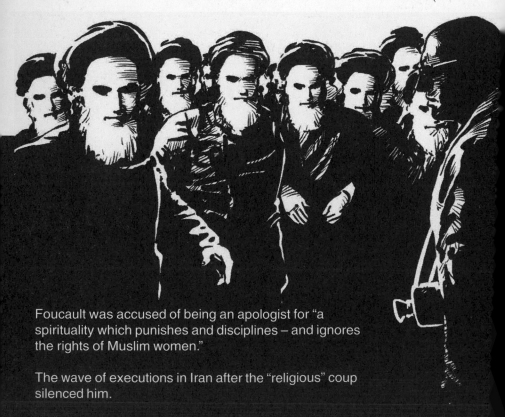

Foucault was accused of being an apologist for "a spirituality which punishes and disciplines – and ignores the rights of Muslim women."

The wave of executions in Iran after the "religious" coup silenced him.

Recidivism

In 1980, Foucault helped to free **Roger Knobelspiess**, who had been banged up in 1972 for allegedly stealing 800 francs. In 1976, he skipped parole, was again captured and accused of several armed robberies, and put in one of the new high-security wings. He wrote his first book, which was prefaced by Foucault. He was pardoned and freed to become a celebrity author.

But I got bored, did another "job" and was imprisoned in 1983.

Bloody embarrassing!

The press talked of the disastrous effects of Foucault's whims.

He was now so involved with issues that he was accused of petitioning everything. Was Foucault overreaching himself?

Against Socialism

In May 1981, the French elected the socialist **François Mitterrand** (1916-96) as President. Foucault's relationship to Socialism was torn apart by its refusal to act on the "internal affair" of martial law being declared in Poland. Foucault, sociologist **Pierre Bourdieu** (b. 1930), writer **Marguerite Duras** (b. 1914), and actor **Yves Montand** (1921-91) signed a petition. The Socialists replied that most intellectuals found it hard to stomach their election victory of 10 May!

Foucault later travelled to Poland in a minibus with members of *Médecins du Monde*, with printing materials to help the cause.

American Fame

Foucault had achieved cult status in the USA. As visiting professor at Berkeley, he lectured in his last years on key areas of his new interests, "Truth and Subjectivity". In October 1979, Foucault was invited to Stanford University in Palo Alto, California.

Time magazine discussed this intellectual who needed police outside the lecture room to prevent overcrowding, but whose work was ignored by traditional historians and philosophers.

Michel Foucault in US and in TIME

TIME

He was even accused, through his work on madness and institutions, of being responsible for unleashing "bag ladies" onto the streets!

WHO'S LETTING
BAG LADIES ON THE STREETS?

Foucault's negative evaluation of the philanthropic dream was coupled with the fashionable claims by English revisionist psychiatrist R.D. Laing that schizophrenia is not a disease.

Back to the Enlightenment

Autumn 1983, Berkeley. Foucault gives a lecture on Immanuel Kant's *What is Enlightenment?* In 1784, Kant saw the Enlightenment as a "way out" of man's immaturity. For the first time, mankind was free from blindly obeying dogma or paying taxes.

Men still have a private duty, but they are now free to reason in public. This is a new moment in history.

It is in the reflection on "today" as difference in history and as a motive for a particular philosophical task that the novelty of this text appears to me to lie.

In the present day, Foucault says, man hasn't yet reached maturity and perhaps never will. But a critical project remains, which means we must ask what we are and analyze historically the limits imposed upon us – so that we may transgress them!

Foucault renounces the quest for truth and plumps for a critical engagement with the present.

Towards Modernity

What comes after the Enlightenment? Is modernity its sequel? Foucault discusses the arch-modern French poet **Charles Baudelaire** (1821-67), who in his work strove to seize the "heroism" of everyday life – the fashion of the present – in the 19th century. But it's not just about seizing the moment.

For the attitude of modernity, the high value of the present is indissociable from a desperate eagerness to imagine it, to imagine it otherwise than it is, and to transform it, not by destroying it, but by grasping it in what it is.

The dandy shows a modern relationship to oneself. He makes himself a work of art.

Modern man doesn't try to find his hidden truth – he invents himself!

The relationship to the self should, therefore, be one of creative and Nietzschean activity of giving style to one's strengths and weaknesses, and not trying to reveal a "true" self.

Baudelaire

Against Foucault

German philosopher and heir to the Frankfurt School of Marxism, **Jürgen Habermas** (b. 1929), attacked Foucault in a 1983 lecture on the "Discourse of Modernity". He'd gone too far.

By getting rid of the possibility of emancipation (from the analyses of oppression and repression in the works of Freud and Marx), Foucault had blunted and blurred any standard of truth. In Foucault's writings, there was no differentiation between knowledge and mystification – just power and discourse.

We still need the Enlightenment's ideal of a rational critique of existing institutions, not just negation. Foucault is neo-conservative, because he supplies no justification for a theoretical alternative to advanced capitalism.

I'm a specific intellectual. I don't stand as master of truth and justice, like you. Universal truth is a mask of power.

Pleasure and its Uses

In 1984, Foucault published the second volume of the *History of Sexuality – The Use of Pleasure*. He takes us back to ancient Greek culture and explores the way in which philosophers and doctors considered rules of conduct in sexual activity. The texts of that time already shape individuals as ethical subjects – each must question his "practices of the self". There are continuities with the modern era, and certain themes which persist even today.

For **Plato** (427-347 BC), sexual practice was not seen as abnormal. Although in the *Laws*, he said sex between men is unnatural, this wasn't a moral judgement about the nature of the act, but its **quantity**.

Too much indulgence is a bad thing. Sexual pleasure, with its intense satisfaction, ensures that people will procreate, and while not bad in itself, it can overshoot its objective. Desire can carry people away!

Some Greek Buzzwords

chresis – the use and management of sexual activity. **Diogenes** (d. 320 BC), the Cynic philosopher, used to masturbate in the market-place to show the public that sexuality was a matter of basic need.

enkrateia – mastery of oneself to become a moral subject. It's a relationship with oneself.
Socrates (469-399 BC):

askesis – exercises in self-control through meditation, fasting and walking the streets in silence, raised the self to a stylization of existence.
Antiphon the Sophist (c. 480-411 BC): "He is not wise who has not tried the ugly and the bad; for then there is nothing that would enable him to assert that he is virtuous."

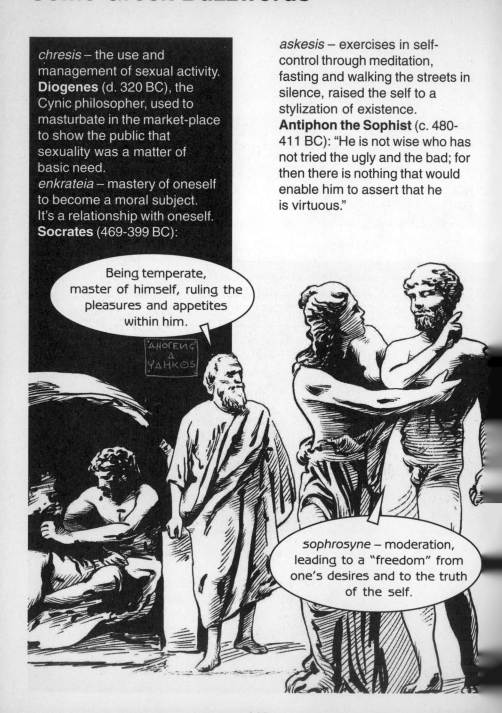

Being temperate, master of himself, ruling the pleasures and appetites within him.

sophrosyne – moderation, leading to a "freedom" from one's desires and to the truth of the self.

Ethical Concerns

The big question Foucault wanted to answer was a simple one. How did sexual behaviour come to be conceived of as a domain of moral experience? He tries to identify fields of ancient Greek practices where the "stylization of the self" was at its most marked.

Aphrodisia – sensual pleasures – are characterized by three ethical concerns in philosophy and law.

1. **Dietetics**. The body and health, or lack of it. Dietetics are rules of conduct. Baths, walking, food and vomiting helped correct excesses. But exercising for its own sake was frowned upon. The environment and temperature were important in regard to sex and to the body's "qualities".

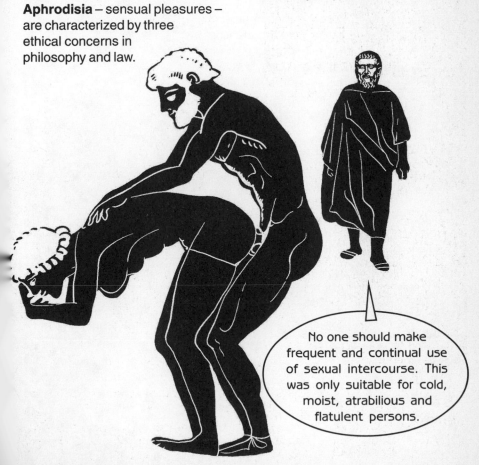

No one should make frequent and continual use of sexual intercourse. This was only suitable for cold, moist, atrabilious and flatulent persons.

2. **Abstention**. Renouncing sexual pleasure is seen as a form of wisdom – as a way of accessing truth.

Households

3. **Economics**, a Greek term originally referring to "households", was concerned with marriage, the role of the wife and extra-marital conduct. A wife's duty was to the husband. He had to respect her but was not restricted sexually just to her. She belonged to him, but he belonged to himself and had to master his authority to preserve the household. It was up to him to make her a "partner" in the household. Any shame she brought on the household would be on account of *his* bad management.

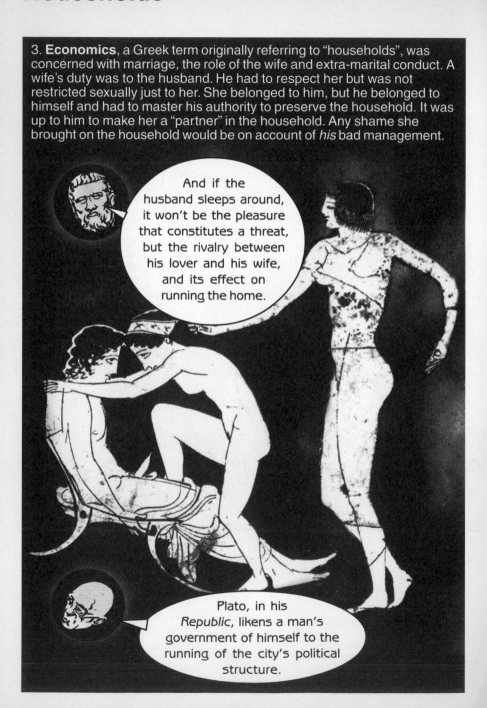

The Love of Boys

Homosexuality, as such, didn't exist in ancient Greece. Categories were different. Love between the same sex and different sexes were not seen as opposites. The *type* of sexual act was irrelevant. Loose morals simply meant being unable to control one's desire for either women or boys. There were not two kinds of desire – just two ways of enjoying pleasure.

I'm a catamite – a boy kept for homosexual purposes.

While homosexuality was condoned by law, it was often treated with scorn. Images of sexuality portrayed the homosexual as effeminate, poncey and vain.

Boys to Men

But why the moral concern, even in Ancient Greece?

Because desire towards boys or women demanded certain ways of behaving.

Between man and boy, there are rules of engagement. The suitor has responsibilities – to restrain himself or to bestow gifts.

The courted boy does not yield too quickly, or lead the man on too long, or look cheap.

Once the boy got too old, the relationship was improper unless it was converted into *philia* – **friendship**. Relationships were tests of honour and *aidos* – **dignity**. Successful conduct would assure good status.

The Relation to Truth

Sexual activity and its relation to truth was developed primarily in relation to the love of boys, not women as later in the Christian period. Truth was not phrased in relation to the object of love, but to *love itself*, and to the soul.

It is not the other half of himself that the individual seeks in the other person; it is the truth to which his soul is related – the hidden medium of his love.

Foucault's conclusion: the ancient Greeks' sexual ethics had inequalities, but were problematized in thought as a relationship between the exercise of a man's freedom, the forms of his power and his access to truth.

The Return of the Subject?

Strange, isn't it? Despite all of Foucault's attempts to get rid of the human individual, to see everything as discourse, apparatus, power and institutions, he still refers to the most anthropological of themes: sexuality, the self, individualization and self-control or will. Is he having his cake and eating it?

Foucault's view of gay Antiquity was not completely positive...

There was too much virility.

An obsession with penetration, and a kind of threat of being dispossessed of your own energy ... All that is quite disgusting!

Foucault was totally against the notion that through sex you could discover the "true self" – hence his avowed anti-Californian stance (despite the fun he had in 'Frisco).

The Care of the Self

In 1982, Foucault lectured on the **hermeneutics of the subject** (hermeneutics means interpretation). This concerned itself with the care of the self and Plato's dialogue *Alcibiades*, in which Alcibiades debates with the virtuous Socrates.

Alcibiades realized that he must care for himself, if he subsequently wanted to care for others.

One must, throughout one's entire life, be one's own project.

The Care of the Self became the title of Foucault's third – and as it turned out, final – volume of the *History of Sexuality*. It focused on the first two centuries AD in the Hellenic and Roman world – and the new importance of the married couple, political roles and civic duties. The cultivation of the self is a response to these changes in a new **stylistics of existence**.

The Cultivation of the Self

In later Antiquity, sexual acts were seen as an anxiety which intensified one's relationship to oneself. One was the subject of one's acts and cultivated oneself. This early Christian cultivation of the self was not more restricted or austere than the Greek version, but had a different emphasis.

Now self-cultivation is built more on the individual, and to an art of living based on universal principles of nature and reason, which *everyone* must observe – whatever their social status.

The regimen of sexual acts was not concerned with morals, but with expenditure of strength.

Oneirocriticism: Looking at Dreams

Artemidorus (c. 150 AD) interpreted dreams in terms of a daily practice of the self – not through moral guidance but simply through **decipherment**. Sexual acts were *not* moral or immoral in themselves – but dreaming about certain acts represented good or bad *omens*. "Sexual dreams foretell the dreamer's destiny in social life … they anticipate the role that he will play in the theatre of family life, professional endeavour, and civic affairs."

If slaves dreamt of masturbating their owner, they would in real life be sentenced by him to a whipping. Economics and the law are read off from dreams.

Getting Married

In Rome, public authority took hold of marriage. Adultery was still an ethical concern, but was now under the jurisdiction of public power, not familial conduct. Marriage was less an economic and political strategy than a voluntary union for all classes – including slaves. It was not a public institution, yet it entailed obligations between the married couple, isolating them more effectively. The **conjugal relationship** was born.

You cannot believe how much I miss you. I love you so much, and we are not used to separations.

Pliny the Younger (61 - 112 AD) shows how passion became introduced as discourse in his letters to his wife when he was away travelling.

The earlier Greek habitual functions of privilege and status are out – this is a love thing!

This is a **relational** marriage – not just about power over oneself, but relation to others.

The Political Self

Retreat into the care of the self does not imply the loss of a wider political, social or civic scene and the individual's relationship to it. The commitment of self to this area needed a greater understanding of how to balance "withdrawal" with "commitment", in order to find the purpose of a man's existence in and out of the home.

One's commitment to politics, to the trappings of power and status, were no longer hard and fast. Power was not about fulfilling duties to others and to the state, or being born into power, but about *governing the self* (constant work!) through reason.

Seneca the Younger (4 BC - 65 AD)

This is particular to each man, whatever his political position.

Each man acquires his character for himself, but accident assigns his duties.

The Body and the Self

Medicine in Rome of the early Christian era was not just concerned with illness and cure. It was a regimen of conduct in all areas: the house, bathing, the environment, the time of day or season. One had to attend to oneself and the state one was generally in.

The sexual act, of course, was an object of interest in its relation to reproduction, the pathology of excretion, to death and diseases.

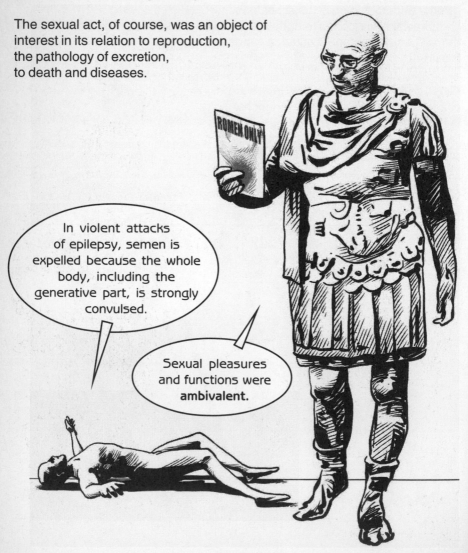

In violent attacks of epilepsy, semen is expelled because the whole body, including the generative part, is strongly convulsed.

Sexual pleasures and functions were **ambivalent**.

Sex was neither a duty nor an evil. Our sperm allows us to cheat death, and sex is natural; yet ejaculation is wasteful and weakens. Like sickness.

The Regimens

Foucault makes the point that although sexual acts were under a careful regimen, they were not seen as moral issues. They were simply *harmful* if improperly practised, according to **Galen** (131-200 AD), the physician.

1. **Procreation**. Take care to prepare the act in body and soul. Allow the sperm to gather strength and have an image of your child in your mind before you procreate.

2. **The age of the subject**. Pleasure must not be continued at old age or begun too early. Girls must menstruate before losing virginity.

3. **The favourable time**.
Plutarch (46-120 AD) advised not
to have sex in the morning.

Because there
may still be ill-digested
food in the stomach – all
the superfluities have not
yet been evacuated
through the urine and
faeces.

Plutarch

4. **Individual
temperaments**.
Constitutions should be
readied for sex through diet
(chick-peas for heat, grapes
for moisture) and exercises.

But no javelin-throwing: the
nutritive material goes to
the wrong parts!

The Work of the Soul

The soul had a dual role to play in sexual practice. It regulated the needs of the body, according to its tensions, and worked to correct errors in itself.

The body did not live up to the purity of the soul. In fact, the soul had to obey the natural mechanics of the body and not overreach the body's desire. The **animal** is the best role-model because sex follows the dictates of the body – of excretion and discharge – not the *doxa* or (popular) belief that pleasure is good.

Images – *phantasia* – are distrusted, as they can stimulate empty desires in the soul.

Satyriasis and *nymphomania* – the male and female extremes of overpowering sexual desire – can be overcome, if you take the advice of **Rufus of Ephesus**.

Sleep on your side rather than on your back. That'll be 100 denarii please.

Imperfect Boys – or a Nice Wife?

Plutarch's *Dialogue on Love* contrasts the love of boys with the love of women in marriage. The question: which one should one choose? In order to compare them, the debate assumes a common ground for love – a **unitary erotics**.

Plutarch borrows from the love of boys its traditional Greek features – restraint and friendship – to show how they apply to the marriage relationship alone.

Boy-love is now imperfect love. Why? Because the love of boys is unharmonious: physical love and true love are imbalanced.

Charis or consenting, reciprocal, intimate love is absent in the potentially **active-passive** man-boy relationship. The old Greek idea of restraint is not valid in this new ethics of mutual love.

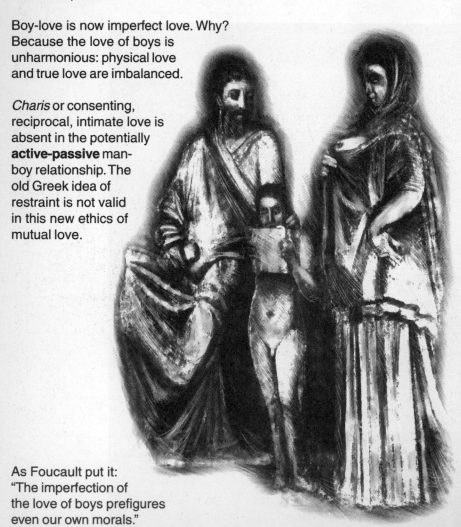

As Foucault put it: "The imperfection of the love of boys prefigures even our own morals."

Don't be Scared

The critical impact of the book was eclipsed by Foucault's sudden illness. In a 1983 interview with Paul Rabinow and Hubert Dreyfus, Greek sex was discussed.

Q. "What about someone who had sex so much he damaged his health?"

A. "That's *hubris*, that's excess. The problem is not one of deviancy but of excess or moderation."

In Berkeley, Foucault discussed AIDS with a student over coffee.

Good luck. And don't be scared!

You too! Don't you be scared.

Don't cry for me if I die.

Foucault was bemused that the AIDS community turned to authority – doctors and religion – for guidance. And further: "How can I be scared of AIDS, when I could die in a car? If sex with a boy gives me pleasure ..."

Foucault developed a severe cough on his return to France, and complained of dizzy spells and constant headaches.

The Death of an Author

On 2 June 1984, Foucault collapsed at home and was taken to the Clinique Saint-Michel, then to Salpêtrière on 9 June. Defert thought he would recover, and Foucault did for a short while. He complained when he couldn't watch the tennis match between John McEnroe and Ivan Lendl on TV because of his treatment.

Le Monde

fr.60

du texte permet de générer de la parole

The Death of an Author

He received visitors and made up with old friends, including Deleuze. Foucault even made plans to sail to the South China Sea to rescue Vietnamese boat people.

On 24 June, Foucault's fever worsened. At 1.15 p.m. on 25 June 1984, Foucault died. He was 57.

All of Foucault's friends were present at his funeral on 29 June, when Gilles Deleuze read from the introduction to the *Use of Pleasures*. A wreath was sent by Polish exiles. Foucault's coffin was taken to Vendeuve-du-Poitou, where he was buried. Foucault's mother lived another two years.

World of tennis

L'usage de la parole est naturel et ne nécessite donc pas d'apprentissage supplémentaire. Ce canal de communication lecture de messagerie, commentaires sonores, à partir du texte permet fonctionne en parallèle avec les autres, oeil, ou main, donc en supplément si ceux ci sont déjà commentaires sonores, traitement de

AIDS

Did Foucault know he had AIDS? It is very likely. He certainly discussed it with friends, but never publicly declared it.

The doctor's press release said that antibiotics had failed to treat infection in the brain – septicaemia.

Foucault Special

On 27 June, *Le Monde* put his death on the front page and published his last text – a plea for the liberation of two Frenchmen imprisoned in Poland. The weekend edition of *Libération* ran a "Foucault special".

Jean-Paul Aron (b. 1925) came out and spoke of his own illness, and criticized the late Foucault for not doing so, to much controversy.

Defert founded AIDES, a self-help AIDS group.

Unfinished Work

Foucault refused to allow a fourth volume, *Confessions of the Flesh*, about desire in the early centuries of Christianity, to be posthumously published, as well as work on Manet. Give it time …

Hervé Guibert's novel, *To The Friend Who Did Not Save My Life*, was supposedly about Foucault's life (as "Muzil") with AIDS. The novel describes San Franciscan houses where men sat in baths which doubled as urinals, cannibalized trucks which became "torture chambers", and Foucault's realization of his fate.

Guibert died in 1991 by suicide with an anti-AIDS drug. In the novel, Stéphane is Daniel Defert and Marine is actress Isabelle Adjani.

After Muzil's death, Stéphane finds a bag full of whips, handcuffs, leather hoods and S & M gear.

A cancer that would hit only homosexuals, no, that's too good to be true, I could just die laughing!

Muzil adored violent orgies in saunas.

166

Foucault Dissected

Foucault had always been dogged by criticism. Here are some generally negative views.

> His work is spectacular, but has little historical accuracy and shows patchy research. He just goes on instinct.

> His style is imperious and doubt-ridden at the same time, a method which supports sweeping summary with eccentric detail.

Response: *He researched, but in a way that told of a less complacent and more open view of history. He identified new problems, new approaches and new objects for the subject.*

The American "postmodern" philosopher, **Richard Rorty** (b. 1931): "Foucault subverts quasi-metaphysical comfort."

Criticism: *He tries to be faithful to each age, relies on documents to support his thesis, yet has contempt for objective truth. But he was the first to claim that the evidence was on his side!*

Foucault Loses

The American Marxist philosopher **Fredric Jameson**: "Foucault has a 'winner loses' logic. The more powerful the vision of a total system becomes, the more powerless the reader feels. Any resistance seems trivial."

Foucault is on the horns of a dilemma: if he is telling the truth about the impossibility of detached truth, then all truth is suspect. But if this is the case, then Foucault's truth cannot vouch for its *own* truth.

Response: *He supplies a new paradigm (model) for the human sciences, imposing some order on the chaos of reason. Where would we be without his **power/knowledge** view of Enlightenment and modernity?*

Contradictions

If Foucault believes that truth and reason are simply effects of power, and that there is no ground – just discourse, the apparatus, institutions, etc. – then he loses, because he wants his theories to be accepted as true. How can Foucault be true and history not be?

Once you dispense with the idea of man as Foucault does, what is there to fight for? Even Nietzsche was more optimistic than Foucault on this point.

He's too harsh on the Enlightenment. He saw nothing good about the 18th century, its critical reflection on itself, its progress, its reason.

It colours his view of modernity as well.

Naive Politics?

Richard Rorty: "Foucault's so-called anarchism is self-indulgent radical chic – his politics tied itself up with pleasure and a **decentred** approach to power. Power as such loses its meaning in his work."

Clifford Geertz (b. 1926), anthropologist: "Foucault was an impossible object – a non-historical historian, an anti-humanistic human scientist, and a counter-structuralist structuralist."

People have banalized his project.

It only took three weeks to convert my book into the slogan, "sexuality has never been repressed".

Foucault In Memoriam

Foucault has left a great legacy – but a flawed one. His increasing cult status and political over-commitment overshadow his academic contribution. Leaving aside his refusal to discuss the media, mass culture and things less classically based, one can ask – did Foucault burn out?

Foucault's death? Loss of confidence in his own genius. Leaving the sexual aspects aside, the loss of the immune system is no more than the biological transcription of the other process.

Baudrillard

Endless "Foucault" conferences abound in the soft political world of postmodern academia. "A discourse on power and on the power of discourse – what is more attractive to intellectuals and humanities departments who are embattled but are sick of dogma?"

Return of the Dead

Foucault's work is used dutifully and unimaginatively by art historians, feminist cultural theorists and political theorists of the disenfranchized Left. Far from a liberation from reason, his work has become a straitjacket.

And he has often been too highly praised. The man is almost a saint to some thinkers. No wonder, when his work superficially seems to fit any inquiry involving knowledge or power, while giving a convenient methodological gloss to modern and postmodern debates.

So the **Foucault industry** is now also a discursive formation – although his ideas have lost the lustre of their 1960s and 70s radicalism. **Foucault-speak** today is only used to prop up tired or politically correct versions of history.

Is this what Michel Foucault would have wanted?

I only wanted to be a goldfish!

Selected Further Reading

Works by Michel Foucault

Madness and Civilization – a History of Insanity in the Age of Reason; USA: Random, 1988; UK: Routledge, 1990

The Order of Things: an Archaeology of the Human Sciences; USA: Random, 1994; UK: Routledge, 1990

The Archaeology of Knowledge; USA: Pantheon, 1982; UK: Routledge, 1990

I, Pierre Rivière, Having Slaughtered my Mother, my Sister and my Brother…; USA & UK: University of Nebraska Press, 1975

Discipline and Punish: the Birth of the Prison; USA: Pantheon, 1977; UK: Penguin, 1991

The History of Sexuality
Volume I: Introduction; USA: Random, 1990; UK: Penguin, 1990
Volume II: the Use of Pleasure; USA: Random, 1990; UK: Penguin, 1988
Volume III: the Care of the Self; USA: Random, 1988; UK: Penguin, 1990

The Birth of the Clinic: an Archaeology of Medical Perception; USA: Random, 1990; UK: Routledge, 1990

Death and the Labyrinth: the World of Raymond Roussel; USA: Doubleday, 1987; UK: Athlone Press, 1987

This is Not a Pipe; USA & UK: University of California Press, 1982

Interviews and Essays

Power/Knowledge: Selected Interviews and Other Writings, 1972-77, ed. Colin Gordon; USA: Pantheon, 1980; UK: Harvester, 1981

Foucault Live: Interviews, 1966-84, ed. Sylvère Lotringer; USA: Semiotext(e), 1989

Language, Counter-Memory, Practice: Selected Essays and Interviews, ed. Donald Bouchard; USA & UK: Cornell University Press, 1980

The Foucault Reader, ed. Paul Rabinow; USA: Pantheon, 1985; UK: Penguin, 1986. A very useful selection from Foucault's major works, with a clear introduction.

Critiques

Michel Foucault: Beyond Structuralism and Hermeneutics, Hubert L. Dreyfus & Paul Rabinow; UK: Harvester, 1982. Concerned with questions of "subjection".

Foucault, Marxism and History: Mode of Production Versus Mode of Information, Mark Poster; USA & UK: Blackwell, 1984. A Marxist response to Foucault's version of power.

Biographies

Michel Foucault, Didier Eribon; USA & UK: Faber & Faber, 1992. Contains photographs of Foucault and chums.

The Lives of Michel Foucault, David Macey; UK: Hutchinson, 1993. Includes a comprehensive bibliography.

Acknowledgements

Chris would like to thank Zoran, Duncan, Richard and Toby for their help.

Zoran is indebted to all the anonymous cyberspace people for their research and all the real people who helped or were patient with him.

Chris Horrocks studied Cultural History at the Royal College of Art in London. He is a lecturer in History of Art at Kingston University in Surrey. He continues to live in Tulse Hill, South London.

Zoran Jevtic is an illustrator and multimedia author from London. He is involved in animation, Internet publishing and music projects.